Christ's death on the cfoundational leaders of w
one theme. That theme, v.
this soon-to-be global group, was forgiveness. Forgiveness is the hinge on which the Christian faith swings, but it is also one of the most neglected and damaged areas in the body of Christ today. Dr. Kazumba Charles brings a revelation on this matter that will shift your capacity to forgive. *The Weapon of Forgiveness* is a must read for all believers.

Bishop Shawn Patrick Williams D.D.
Founder, Warrior Nations Intl. Fellowship and
Impact School of Ministry and 13 Apostolic Training Centers

These are two of my favorite quotes from the book:

> "If there is a disease that is slowly eating up the church and many believers in Christ, it is offense. There is not a single week goes by that I do not meet a person who has left a church or churches because of offense."
>
> "The enemy's primary tactic is to use offense and unforgiveness to keep us away from the power of God and away from His vision for our lives."

Unforgiveness is probably the most difficult issue we face in the body of Christ, perhaps because of its deceptive nature. Charles does an amazing job of explaining the nuances of unforgiveness—the how, when and why—and how to effectively deal with it in our lives. Charles has written a comprehensive book on the subject of forgiveness, one that makes very clear that we do not have the solid grasp on this subject many of us believe we have. Our ignorance on this matter has effectively hindered God's power, given Satan an advantage over us, and brought weakness to the church. "My people are destroyed for lack of knowledge," the Lord said. In this book we have an awesome opportunity to grow in the knowledge and wisdom of God, to better safeguard our lives against Satan's schemes.

From the first day Charles walked into our church, I have watched him grow and mature into the man of God he has become, and I know it has not been easy. Coming to a foreign country, leaving family and friends behind, and living in a different culture as he sought to fulfil his purpose in life had the potential to create offense. Charles has handled these things brilliantly and is a true testament to the weapon of forgiveness. I highly recommend you read this book and buy a copy to give away. It is well worth it. Your life will be strengthened and empowered. I know mine has!

Pastor Brent Rudoski
Faith Alive Ministries, Canada

In *The Weapon of Forgiveness*, Dr. Kazumba shines a bright light on the importance of forgiveness in our lives. I was impressed with the solid biblical teaching put forward and the accompanying insights about why forgiveness really matters. It is obvious the author has been taught by the Father. This is a good and important book, full of practical insights that will benefit everyone who reads it. I heartily recommend it to you.

John Drisner
Saskatchewan District Superintendent for the Pentecostal Assemblies of Canada
Lead Pastor of The Neighbourhood Church

SPIRITUAL WARFARE, BOOK 1

The WEAPON of FORGIVENESS

Dr. Kazumba Charles

THE WEAPON OF FORGIVENESS
Copyright © 2015 by Dr. Kazumba Charles

All rights reserved. Neither this publication nor any part of this publication may be reproduced or transmitted in any form or by any means, electronic or mechanical, including photocopying, recording or any information storage and retrieval system, without permission in writing from the author.

Unless otherwise indicated, Scripture is taken from the Holman Christian Standard Bible, copyright 1999, 2000, 2002, 2003 by Holman Bible Publishers. Used by permission. • Scripture marked ESV is taken from the Holy Bible, English Standard Version, copyright © 2001 by Crossway Bibles, a division of Good News Publishers. Used by permission. All rights reserved. • Scripture marked ISV is taken from the International Standard Version. Copyright © 1995–2014 by ISV Foundation. All rights reserved internationally. Used by permission of Davidson Press, LLC. • Scripture marked NASB is taken from the New American Standard Bible. Copyright © 1960, 1962, 1963, 1968, 1971, 1972, 1973, 1975, 1977, 1995 by The Lockman Foundation. Used by permission. • Scripture marked NIV is taken from the HOLY BIBLE, NEW INTERNATIONAL VERSION®. NIV®. Copyright © 1973, 1978, 1984 by International Bible Society. Used by permission of Zondervan. All rights reserved. • Scripture marked KJV is taken from the King James Version of the Bible. • Scripture marked NLT is taken from the Holy Bible, New Living Translation, copyright © 1996. Used by permission of Tyndale House Publishers, Inc., Wheaton, IL 60189. All rights reserved.

ISBN: 978-1-4866-1200-0

Word Alive Press
131 Cordite Road, Winnipeg, MB R3W 1S1
www.wordalivepress.ca

Cataloguing in Publication information may be obtained through Library and Archives Canada

Acknowledgments — vii
Foreword — ix
Introduction — xi

1: FORGIVENESS — 1
2: THE MYSTERIOUS POWER OF FORGIVENESS — 17
3: THE POWER OF YOUR TONGUE — 31
4: OFFENSE: A BAIT OF THE DEVIL — 47
5: EFFECTIVE WAYS TO DEAL WITH OFFENSE — 65
6: THE DANGERS OF UNFORGIVENESS — 79
7: THE WEAPON OF FORGIVENESS — 93
8: WHY FORGIVE? — 109
9: EFFECTUAL FORGIVENESS — 123
10: THE POWER OF RECONCILIATION — 139

Conclusion — 151
About the Author — 157

Acknowledgments

FIRST AND FOREMOST, I WOULD LIKE TO ACKNOWLEDGE MY LORD AND MASTER, JESUS Christ, and express my appreciation for empowering me to be a passionate ambassador of the gospel of the kingdom of God to the nations. Without Him, this would not have been possible. It is because of His passion and love for souls and for His people that I write this book. I also would like to acknowledge my greatest Companion, who gave me insight, wisdom, and revelation on how to write this book to my fellow believers in Christ. His name is the Holy Spirit. I could not have written this book if it had not been for His inspiration and presence in my life.

I also would like to recognize the great blessing of my life, my partner in ministry, a great mother, and a powerful woman of God: my wife, Glory Kassimu Kazumba. Our life indeed has been a great journey of faithfulness to God's calling because of her support, love, and dedication to winning souls for God's kingdom. I am forever grateful to you, Glory. May the glory of God keep shining on your face. To my daughters, Louriana and Briona, and to my son, Joshua McCharles, I say thank you, guys, for your love for God and for Daddy and Mammy. You are special to us.

Finally, I would like to recognize a few people who have had a great impact and spiritual influence upon my life; namely, my mother, Juliet Kabwe Kazumba, for laying a strong biblical foundation in my life; my late father, Mr. Kazumba, for teaching me how to love people; and Dr.

David and Mrs. Joyce Pierce for supporting us, mentoring us, teaching us, and being there for us when we first moved to Canada to study the Word of God and for being such great examples to us of what it means to love and serve God.

And I can't forget the many men and women of God who have spoken into my life over the years and encouraged me to go for God wholeheartedly, including our church family, our faithful and true friends in ministry, who have supported and partnered with us for many years. Without your support, it would be impossible for us to do what God has called us to do—winning souls for His kingdom. Your love and support is highly appreciated, and we thank God for you. May He continue to bless you and watch over you and your households.

Foreword

THERE ARE MANY SPIRITUAL WEAPONS GOD HAS GIVEN US FOR OUR ARSENAL TO FIGHT AND wage war against the enemy. None is more important than the weapon of forgiveness. When it comes to forgiveness, it doesn't matter *who* is right but *what* is right. Forgiveness is always the right thing to do, regardless of what hurt has been imposed on our lives. Dr. Kazumba Charles is a man of God who has traveled the world preaching the gospel of Jesus Christ and offering a message that includes the power of forgiveness. In this book, you will learn what forgiveness is, and you will also learn what forgiveness is not. Open your heart and allow this inspired truth of forgiveness to penetrate your life. Use the "weapon of forgiveness" to bring victory in your life and set you up for success.

Pastor Bill Jenkins
Church of Acts
Indianapolis, Indiana USA
www.churchofacts.org

Introduction

THIS BOOK COVERS TEN VERY IMPORTANT TOPICS THAT WILL CHANGE AND REVOLUTIONIZE your life: Forgiveness, the mystery power of forgiveness, the power of your tongue, offense, effective ways to deal with offense, the dangers of unforgiveness, the weapon of forgiveness, why we should forgive, effectual forgiveness, and the power of reconciliation. The power and anointing of God revealed in the discussion of these topics will set you on a path to your breakthrough and victory—victory that begins with forgiveness.

Life is like a mixture of salt and sugar. Sometimes it is full of great and wonderful experiences, and sometimes it is full of sorrow, sadness, and tears. Sometimes you find good, loving, kind, gentle, and caring people, and sometimes you meet hateful, angry, offensive, abusive, bitter, and resentful people who do everything possible to destroy your day and your testimony for Christ. Jesus and many other great characters of the Bible experienced the same things, but they did not allow demonically inspired battles to distract them from their God-given mission and purpose on earth. They knew Satan was behind every attack because he did not want them to fulfill their kingdom mission. Think of a man of God like Nehemiah. He was ridiculed, opposed, mocked, intimidated, and called a rebel when he and his people were rebuilding the broken walls of Jerusalem (Nehemiah 3, 4, 6). Nehemiah did not give up or go after his enemies, however. Instead, he turned to God in prayer and asked God to fight for him and his people. After enduring fifty-two days of opposition, Nehemiah and the people completed the building of the walls. And when their enemies, who had been mocking them, heard this, they were intimidated and lost their confidence because they realized God Himself had helped Nehemiah and the people finish the great task of rebuilding Jerusalem's walls.

In life, knowing how to handle and respond to unpleasant moments, opposition, or even rejection is crucial. If you seek to walk powerfully and faithfully with God and demonstrate His character to the world, you must learn to respond properly to the attacks and opposition that will inevitably come. Otherwise, you will be disappointed, defeated, and run over. You will be distracted in your walk with God, and your faith might well be shipwrecked. As a Christian, you need to know who your real enemy is and who your Helper (God) is. You also need to know what weapons you have to fight the enemy. Without this knowledge, you will end up fighting spiritual battles in your own strength and ability, and consequently be badly bruised and defeated. God is your Helper, and the battle belongs to Him. All you need to defeat the enemy are the weapons of forgiveness, prayer, praise, and worship.

The Devil has unleashed his evil spirit of offense upon the earth today. This is why we see many people offended by the church, national leaders, and each other like never before. And through offense, the enemy has somehow managed to sneak hatred, anger, and bitterness into the hearts of many Christians. As a result, believers are failing to allow the power of the Holy Spirit to move in their lives, in the church, and in their families and therefore do not demonstrate God's power to the nations.

Our vessels have been contaminated—that is why we are not seeing the mighty powers of God in our midst. The good news, though, is that God wants to decontaminate each and every one of us from bitterness and anger and empower us with His love, mercy, and grace and with a powerful weapon Satan cannot withstand: The weapon of forgiveness.

It is quite evident in the world today that many people (Christians included) are not happy, simply because they have been offended or feel offended. Many Christians are not progressing spiritually as they should because of what happened to them, or what somebody did to them, or what somebody said or did not say to them. At the center of this strife and unhappiness is the evil force of *unforgiveness*. It is extremely important for us Christians to understand that unforgiveness is a powerful weapon Satan uses against us to poison our lives and futures. It locks us up in the shackles of depression, sin, death, and problems of all kinds. Where there is unforgiveness, there is hatred, jealousy, factions, envy, revenge, and prejudice. In fact, unforgiveness has caused many people to turn away from God, church, friends, and families, and prevented God from moving powerfully in churches around the world.

Unforgiveness is a wrong response to offense. Offense is the chief catalyst of anger, and anger produces unforgiveness, and unforgiveness leads to ungodly acts. Offense and anger are poisonous seeds that can develop into a tree of unforgiveness. Because of offense, many people have lost their fire, passion, and love for Jesus Christ. They have allowed offense and disappointments to disconnect them from Jesus Christ, the only source of all life and blessings. Countless people, both in the church and in the world, are living in disappointment, bitterness, and anger due to offense. Indeed, we see life after life, marriage after marriage, and church after church destroyed by the power of offense and bitterness.

The divine and powerful weapon of forgiveness, however, can protect your life, future, ministry, and marriage as you live in a world full of disappointments and offense. Forgiveness brings great devastation into the enemy's camp and creates a way for God's people to walk in unity, victory, joy, and happiness and to experience the power of God. Furthermore, forgiveness is an evangelistic tool that can help us win souls and advance the kingdom of God. We cannot effectively preach the good news of God's grace with unforgiving hearts that are full of bitterness and anger.

Forgiving your enemy does not mean you are weak or a loser; rather, it sends a strong signal or message of victory to your enemies, even as it releases you from the traps of Satan and sets you on the path designed for you by your heavenly Father—a path of joy in Him and victory because He has overcome the enemy by forgiving *your* sins. Each time you are offended and you forgive, you are shaming the Devil and destroying his tactics. At the same time, you are growing from faith to faith and from glory to glory. In this time in which we are living, God is seeking and preparing a people after His own heart, a people who are merciful, compassionate, and passionate about winning souls for His kingdom and demonstrating His love through forgiving other people.

Will you be one of those people who advance the kingdom of God at such a crucial time as this? Learning about the power of forgiveness and how it can be used as a weapon against the Devil is going to give you the tools you need to advance the kingdom of God and defeat the kingdom of darkness. Through the weapon of forgiveness, you will be able to open doors in your life that seem to be closed and to walk in victory after victory.

Here is one important thing you need to know as you read this life-changing book: The many times you are offended and mistreated can be used by the Devil to bring your life to a standstill or to destroy your life completely if you refuse to forgive those who have offended you. Satan takes every opportunity to sow seeds of bitterness, anger, and unforgiveness. You may have every reason in the world not to forgive the one who has offended you, but understand this: Forgiveness destroys Satan's evil intentions toward us and opens up the influence of the Holy Spirit in our lives to lead us in the ways of God.

In this book, you will discover what forgiveness really means and why it is so difficult to forgive. But you will also learn that forgiving as God forgives brings joy, restoration, new life, hope, blessings, and deeper connection to the power of God. Furthermore, through this book you will learn how to use forgiveness to "unlock" your life and the lives of those who have offended you. You will also learn how to change the spiritual atmosphere around you in your home and in the marketplace. We are called to bless and not to curse (Romans 12:14; Matthew 5:44). Forgiveness is "giving" (blessing), while withholding forgiveness is actually "cursing," or wishing evil upon, someone.

Every person on earth has been offended or hurt by someone, and everyone has also offended or hurt someone else, either knowingly or unknowingly, through words or actions. There is no denying this. In fact, 1 John 1:8 tells us, "If we claim to be without sin, we deceive ourselves and the truth is not in us" (NIV). Yet many people excuse their wrongful deeds or offensive words. Often, we hear them claim, "It was a slip of the tongue" instead of owning up to wrongdoing and doing what is right; namely, asking for forgiveness so that they can be in right standing with both God and man. A "slip of the tongue" actually is an overflow of what is inside the heart. Clean what is in your heart, and you will also clean what comes out of your mouth (cf. Matthew 15:18-20). God wants to clean the hurt, pain, hatred, anger, bitterness, and resentment from our hearts so that He can fill us with genuine love, compassion, and mercy, and we can live as true kingdom people.

Every human being must deal with offense and with forgiving or being forgiven. Yet as we noted before, most people, Christians included, live with chains of bitterness, hatred, anger, and slander around their hearts. If you have been asking yourself why there is so much hatred and war in the world today, the answer is because there are so many people living in the bondage of anger, bitterness, and hatred. And this is because people have become lovers of self, ungrateful, proud, abusive, and arrogant, just as Paul predicted in 2 Timothy 3:2. Everything today centers on one's feelings and not on the needs or concerns of others or on what God's Word says.

The Devil has unleashed the weapon of offense upon the earth today. But we, the people of God, can overturn this by unleashing the weapon of forgiveness against the Devil and take territories for God through love and mercy. Without the atmosphere and spirit of forgiveness, we can never be effective in advancing the kingdom of God, because an unwillingness to forgive is a yoke that weighs down our spiritual effectiveness and gives room to the influence of the Devil. And it creates a stumbling block for others. We would do well to remember Jesus' words in Matthew 18:7: "Woe to the world because of the things that cause people to stumble! Such things must come, but woe to the person through whom they come!" (NIV).

We Christians have been forgiven much by God through the sacrifice of His Son, Jesus Christ. His forgiveness of our many sins should empower us and motivate us to forgive others unconditionally and to love them just as He loves us. Yes, you may have experienced terrible things in your life, but as long as you are still holding a grudge in your heart against the person or persons who wronged you, you are giving Satan dominion over your life. Unforgiveness is a sin; it is evil, destructive, and vicious. We need to confront it, deal with it, and flush it out of our midst before it destroys God's plans for us.

Speaking from experience, I totally understand how difficult it is to forgive and love those who may have wronged, mistreated, and abused you. But when you understand the evil behind unforgiveness and the power of forgiveness, you will uncover Satan's traps and gain victory. When I was going through the storms of injustice in my life, the Lord revealed to me the power of forgiveness. When I forgave all those who had mistreated me, doors began to open in my ministry, one after another. God started using me powerfully wherever I was invited to minister, and He provided unlikely sources of financial support for our ministry. The Lord also spoke to me during the most trying moments of my life and showed me that I was not to do things to prove wrong those who had unfairly treated me but instead to do things because they are the will of God and the right thing to do.

God is the Father of forgiveness. By sending His only begotten Son, Jesus Christ, to die on the cross as the sacrifice and payment for humanity's sins, He demonstrated that He would rather die to save His created people than watch them perish. This character of God was also expressed in Jesus' teaching in the parable of the lost sheep (Luke 15:1–7), the parable of the lost coin (Luke 15:8–10), and the parable of the lost son (Luke 15:11–32).

In this book, it is my desire and passion to help you understand the weapon of forgiveness as God has revealed it to me, so that you can be a victor and not a victim of Satan's snares and thus move to another level in your spiritual life. The time has come to possess what is rightfully yours in the kingdom of God, but this means getting rid of a few things in your life, with God's help.

Those things that can hinder us from walking in the promises of God include unforgiveness, bitterness, anger, pride, hatred, and resentment. Forgiveness is the power that causes us to walk in God's blessings. Through God's forgiveness of our sins, we have received the blessings of eternal life. Forgiveness is a key to unlocking the locked doors in our lives. Indeed, it is a key to reformation, transformation, and real revival. Where there is forgiveness, there is unity, love, and corporate anointing; and where there is unity, love, and corporate anointing, there is the power of God.

Chapter 1
FORGIVENESS

MANY OF US MAY HAVE AN IDEAL OF WHAT FORGIVENESS IS, AND YET WE LACK AN understanding of the power of forgiveness and consequently fail to walk in it every day of our lives. Our constant struggle to forgive other people is a reminder of how we need to deeply understand God's own heart of forgiveness and learn how we can effectively walk in forgiveness. We have not forgiven until we walk in forgiveness and prove it through our acts of love toward the person who has offended us.

One of my desires in this book is to show how we can walk effectively in the power of forgiveness and demonstrate the kingdom of God through forgiveness and love, for, indeed, without these two it is impossible to advance the kingdom of God or to represent God's interests here on earth. God is loving, merciful, gracious, compassionate, and slow to anger (Psalm 145:8; Exodus 34:6; Numbers 14:18). He is not rude or unforgiving, as are some religious people who claim to be God's children. If we want to be real ambassadors of God, we need to begin by forgiving others and being messengers of heavenly peace and love.

We need a deeper understanding of what forgiveness really is from the depths of God's own heart, as demonstrated by His acts of forgiveness recorded in the Bible. God's forgiveness is totally different from the "worldly" concept of forgiveness. Worldly forgiveness has limits and is usually performed in order to be forgiven. God's forgiveness is unlimited and freely given according to the riches of His grace.

In this first chapter, we are going to look at forgiveness from the depth of God's heart and from His deeds of forgiveness. I believe that learning about forgiveness from the Master of forgiveness—God Himself—will help us grasp the magnitude, depth, and power of forgiveness, and this in turn will empower us to use forgiveness as a weapon of spiritual warfare. It is only when we understand God's forgiving heart and forgiveness of our enormous debt of sin that we are able to freely forgive others, regardless of their debt to us.

Once you understand the power of forgiveness and how through forgiveness you can have a breakthrough in life and defeat and destroy the tactics of the Devil, you will never allow the spirit of unforgiveness to occupy your heart again. Forgiveness acts like a doorway to your prayers being answered, to entering into the presence of God, and to walking in the power of God. You can never have your prayers answered when you have unforgiveness in your heart. Furthermore, you cannot enter into the presence of God or walk in His power without His forgiving you first, but He can't forgive you if you won't forgive other people (cf. Matthew 6:14–15; 18:27–35). Forgiveness, therefore, is crucial to your relationship with God, His Son Jesus Christ, and the Holy Spirit, as well as with the people God created in His image. Satan's goal is to use offense and hurt to fuel bitterness and anger in the hearts of people so that he can get them to withhold forgiveness and thereby destroy their fellowship and relationship with God. Forgiveness is your secret weapon and the key to entering into your new season of God's blessings and anointing.

The Meaning of Forgiveness

What is forgiveness, according to God? What does it look like? First, as a Christian, it is important to understand that forgiveness is not simply excusing a fault, denying a wrong that has been committed against you, forgetting the wrong as if it were never committed, or giving up the pursuit of vengeance against the one who has hurt you. These are shallow and worldly standards of forgiveness and are part of the reason so many people in the world struggle to effectively forgive those who offend or hurt them. Godly forgiveness is deeper and more powerful than these ideas because it is directly connected to love for God and for His created people, the two most important commandments of God: "You shall love the Lord your God with all your heart and with all your soul and with all your strength and with all your mind, and your neighbor as yourself" (Luke 10:27 ESV; cf. Matthew 22:34–40). Godly forgiveness is not driven by hurt but instead by love. If a person claims to love God, he or she must also demonstrate that love for God by forgiving and loving other people.

To help us define forgiveness, we must look at the Hebrew word *nasa*. The word *nasa* simply means to take up, carry, bear, or lift. When used in relation to forgiveness, the idea is that God pardoned our sins by *taking them up* and laying them on His sinless Son, Jesus Christ, who *carried* or *lifted* our sins to the cross. Sin, which dominated each one of us, was taken up by Jesus and taken away from us. God's forgiveness means God takes up our sins and carries the penalty away from us because of His love for us, His created people. He hasn't forgiven us because of what we have done or because we deserve to be forgiven but because of His deep, unconditional love for us. His passionate love has washed our sins away and lifted them up away from us. This is why the Bible says, "Love covers over a multitude of sins" and over "all wrongs" (1 Peter 4:8; Proverbs 10:12 NIV). Forgiveness that flows from love restores, revives, and renews, and it is effective because it is done God's way. Forgiveness done any other way is not forgiveness. You have not forgiven until you can love and lend a helping hand to your enemy.

To help us expound more on what forgiveness means according to God and how it is acted out, let us turn to the book of Luke. In Luke 10:25–37, Jesus shared a very important parable about a Samaritan who helped a man who had been beaten and left to die. Jesus' story presents a great example of what forgiveness done out of love for God and for one's neighbor really looks like.

> *Just then an expert in the law stood up to test Him, saying, "Teacher, what must I do to inherit eternal life?" "What is written in the law?" He asked him. "How do you read it?" He answered: "Love the Lord your God with all your heart, with all your soul,*

with all your strength, and with all your mind; and your neighbor as yourself." "You've answered correctly," He told him. "Do this and you will live." But wanting to justify himself, he asked Jesus, "And who is my neighbor?" Jesus took up the question and said: "A man was going down from Jerusalem to Jericho and fell into the hands of robbers. They stripped him, beat him up, and fled, leaving him half dead. A priest happened to be going down that road. When he saw him, he passed by on the other side. In the same way, a Levite, when he arrived at the place and saw him, passed by on the other side. But a Samaritan on his journey came up to him, and when he saw the man, he had compassion. He went over to him and bandaged his wounds, pouring on olive oil and wine. Then he put him on his own animal, brought him to an inn, and took care of him. The next day he took out two denarii, gave them to the innkeeper, and said, 'Take care of him. When I come back I'll reimburse you for whatever extra you spend.' "Which of these three do you think proved to be a neighbor to the man who fell into the hands of the robbers?" "The one who showed mercy to him," he said. Then Jesus told him, "Go and do the same."

In Sunday schools and in sermons, the parable of the good Samaritan has been taught countless times, yet very few people understand how deeply the parable is connected to effective forgiveness. Jesus was not teaching a story about kind actions, even though such actions certainly are present in the story. Rather, He was teaching a kingdom principle that all kingdom people must grasp and live by here on earth. In order for us to understand this parable, we need to look at the relationship between the Samaritan and the man who was left half dead. Who were the Samaritans? Samaritans were descended from a mixture of Israelites and people from various other nations that the conquering Assyrians resettled in Samaria, as recorded in 2 Kings 17. The Samaritans practiced an offshoot of Judaism and rejected the temple in Jerusalem as a legitimate place of worship.

Jewish people and Samaritans did not think well of one another (cf. Matthew 10:5; John 4:9). The Jews considered the Samaritans "false worshipers" as well as enemies. For such an enemy to show compassion, love, mercy, and forgiveness to a badly injured Jew reveals the condition and content of the Samaritan's heart. God's love was in him. There is no doubt this Samaritan, though looked down upon by Jews, understood the most basic principle of God's law: "Love the Lord your God with all your heart and with all your soul and with all your strength and with all your mind, and your neighbor as yourself." Obviously it was this principle, which was ingrained in his heart, that led the Samaritan not only to rescue the half-dead man but also to pay the bill at an inn for his care.

The priest and the Levite, who were both Jewish, should have come to the aid of this man, but they passed by on the other side, obviously fearful of becoming ritually unclean. However, the Samaritan took a risk, put aside his differences with the Jewish people, and demonstrated Yahweh's character and nature by *lifting off* his offense at the Jews, *taking up* the responsibility of rescuing the man, *carrying* the man to an inn, and *bearing the cost,* or bill, upon himself. That is true forgiveness. The Samaritan proved to be a good neighbor by his gracious actions toward the man who had been attacked. Most people would be happy to see their enemy harmed, but a godly person cannot stand seeing a human being suffering and will rush to the rescue. Enemy or no enemy—God's love is bigger than offense and hurts, and it covers a multitude of sins. To inherit the kingdom of God, or demonstrate the rule and reign of God's kingdom here on earth, we must have love and an attitude of forgiveness.

In a nutshell, forgiveness simply means to let go, to remit, or to give up a debt by not demanding it or keeping it any longer. Forgiveness unloads the hurt, bitterness, and anger and releases them from your system. When you forgive your offenders, you benefit not only in the life to come but also in this present life because a healthy relationship with others will significantly improve both your physical and your spiritual condition. Don't withhold forgiveness, and don't make forgiveness dependent upon your offender's repentance. Let go of your offense, and don't demand payback or revenge.

If You Truly Love and Fear God, You Will Surely Forgive Your Enemies

As a disciple of Jesus Christ, forgiveness, love, mercy, and grace should be evident in your response to people who have offended you. Your love for and fear of God should be motivating factors in forgiving others. We forgive because of the power of God's love that is birthed in our hearts through God's forgiveness of our sins. Let your love and forgiveness go beyond your race, creed, nationality, and social background. Forgive and love people because human beings are worth being cared for and loved. Your forgiveness and love should never be restricted only to people who look like you or share the same nationality or faith. Forgiveness should be shown to all humanity because God's love is without borders or boundaries.

Proverbs 17:9 says, "Whoever would foster love covers over an offense, but whoever repeats the matter separates close friends" (NIV). The love of God in us is what stimulates and cultivates forgiveness for those who have offended us. Our strength to forgive flows from our love for God and God's love for us. People who struggle to forgive are lacking in godly love and knowledge of who God really is. They may have knowledge *about* who God is and know of His works, but they don't know His ways, character, and nature. The ways of God are seen in His love, mercy, grace, and forgiveness.

Forgiving other people's faults is essential to a proper relationship with God and man. We are a blessed and righteous people of God because Jesus Christ *took up* our sins, and the consequences of them, upon Himself—like the Good Samaritan who took the responsibilities of the bill upon himself. Today we are a forgiven people because God extended His love and mercy to us and forgave our sins while we were still sinners. "Blessed is he whose transgression is forgiven, whose sin is covered" (Psalm 32:1 KJV), the psalmist wrote. God doesn't want us just to enjoy His forgiveness of our sins; He wants us to extend forgiveness to those who offend, or sin against, us. We are to lift the pain of being offended to the cross and pardon our offenders so that we can live in peace with both them and our God and move forward in life. We have not truly forgiven until we extend love and mercy to our enemies and pray for them.

Forgiveness is a very big, important, and biblical theme for us Christians and the church in general to explore, study, and practically implement in our day-to-day walk with God and with people. Forgiveness is strongly connected to love. We cannot walk in love without walking in forgiveness, and we cannot walk in forgiveness without walking in love. First John 4:20 tell us, "Whoever claims to love God yet hates a brother or sister is a liar. For whoever does not love their brother and sister, whom they have seen, cannot love God, whom they have not seen" (NIV). True Christians, or disciples of Jesus Christ, love God the Father and love people. Of course, the truth is that it is difficult to love people, especially if they have wronged us, opposed us, hurt us, or persecuted us. Still, we need to clearly understand that we cannot claim to love God if we hate the very people God created in His image.

I cannot emphasize enough that our love for God is not separate from our love for people. God says if we cannot love the people we see with our own eyes, how can we love Him whom we have never seen with our naked eyes? Let us always remember this: We forgive not because people deserve our forgiveness but out of love for God, who has forgiven us. We demonstrate His love and forgiveness over our life by loving and forgiving people. God has given us a new life through the power of forgiveness, and we ought to demonstrate it. Without walking in the power of forgiveness, it is impossible for us to accurately represent the kingdom of God and to make an impact in the world. Forgiveness not only demonstrates our connection with God and appreciation for what He has done for us but it is also a weapon that destroys the Devil's tactics. When we learn to forgive, we discover how to walk in the supernatural and impossible.

My prayer is that as you read this book you will discover the weapon of forgiveness and effectively use it to destroy all the stumbling blocks Satan has set up in your life through offense, anger, and bitterness. We all know that forgiveness is a powerful instrument that brings reconciliation and restoration in relationships, marriages, and church families and also helps in rebuilding or mending trust, faith, and unity between people. But what many of us have failed to see is that forgiveness is actually a weapon infused with the supernatural power of God to defeat and disarm Satan's evil plans, bring both physical and spiritual healing and freedom into our lives, and cause us to focus more on God's plans for our lives than on the pain or evil that offense can bring into our hearts. Forgiveness is not a casual or emotional act. It is something we do thoughtfully with a clear conscience, knowing that as we forgive, we are using the weapon of God to break down the power of Satan's influence over our lives and over the lives of the offenders. If we refuse to forgive others, then we are actually using the Devil's weapon of unforgiveness to hold people in the prison of their own sins and to imprison ourselves to the spirit of bitterness and anger, which eventually controls us and leads us to evil actions against others.

Satan uses his weapon of unforgiveness to destroy the body of Christ, people's visions and dreams in life, and godly relationships. His goal is to cause people to focus on their hurts (i.e., self-worship) and on the offender instead of focusing on God and His purpose for their lives. In this book, it is my goal to help you discover, or rediscover, the weapon of forgiveness for your day-to-day spiritual warfare so that you can move forward in your life, defeat the tricks of the enemy, and demonstrate the true heart of our forgiving God. The enemy hates it when we forgive others. His goal is to influence us to seek revenge and take matters into our own hands so that we will be partakers of his evil deeds and not demonstrate the unconditional love, forgiveness, grace, and mercy that reflects the true nature of God (cf. Luke 6:36).

Forgiveness also has a bearing on our worship. God's throne is governed by His righteousness, mercy, justice, and forgiveness (cf. Psalm 89:14). When we come to the "altar," or into the presence of the only true and living God, to offer the sacrifice of praise, we need to come with a spirit and attitude of forgiveness. Forgiving and showing mercy toward others is extremely important in the kingdom of God. In fact, God cannot accept our sacrifice or forgive our sins if we are not willing to forgive others. Mark 11:25 tells us that when we stand praying, if we hold anything against anyone, we must forgive them, so that our Father in heaven may forgive our sins. Forgiveness is the key to the door of breakthrough in life. With it we can force open any doors that seem to be closed by the enemy.

Forgiving people is not an easy task. Each one of us can testify that it is indeed difficult to forgive those who have done us wrong. One of the reasons forgiving others is so difficult and a constant battle is because Satan fights to keep us in the bondage of unforgiveness so that he can control us. As long as we are controlled or influenced by bitterness, anger, and hatred, we cannot demonstrate to each other and to the world the pure character of God, which is love.

Two Powerful Weapons: Forgiveness and Love

Jesus commanded His disciples to love one another, even as He had loved them (without keeping an account of their sins). By loving each other, they would demonstrate to the whole world that they were indeed His disciples, or children of God (John 13:34–35). In Mark 12:28–33, Jesus taught His followers, "Love your neighbor as yourself." In Matthew 5:43–48, He expanded on this teaching by telling His followers to love their *enemies* and to pray for them:

> *"You have heard that it was said, Love your neighbor and hate your enemy. But I tell you, love your enemies and pray for those who persecute you, so that you may be sons of your Father in heaven. For He causes His sun to rise on the evil and the good, and sends rain on the righteous and the unrighteous. For if you love those who love you, what reward will you have? Don't even the tax collectors do the same? And if you greet only your brothers, what are you doing out of the ordinary? Don't even the Gentiles do the same? Be perfect, therefore, as your heavenly Father is perfect."*

As Jesus was teaching that day on the mount, the crowd that had gathered to listen were taught not only to love their neighbors as commanded in Leviticus 19:18 but also to love their enemies and persecutors and to pray for them. This was a new and different level of love. These people understood that they were to hate the enemies of God (cf. Psalm 139:19–22; 140:9–11). Who would love an evil and abusive person? And why would somebody show love and kindness to his or her enemies, let alone pray for them? Only a person who has experienced the unconditional love of God would extend love to his or her enemies and pray for them. Loving your enemies and praying for those who have abused and mistreated you demonstrates that you are a true child of God who has been forgiven by Him and consumed by His love.

Jesus told the people to be perfect as God the Father is perfect. Well, we know that it is impossible in our own efforts to live a perfect life, but as we forgive those who have wronged us just as God the Father has forgiven us, we illustrate the perfect love of God in us. Demonstrating unconditional love to our enemies and to others is one of the most important expressions of God's true character in us. To be children of God, we must resemble His character and nature and do what He does perfectly—forgive and love those who don't deserve to be forgiven or loved at all. Forgiveness empowers us to live beyond and above our hurts because we are not of this world but of the kingdom of God. Forgiveness and love are not just requirements of God. They represent a lifestyle, as well as weapons that destroy every obstacle and stronghold in our lives. The first weapon God unleashed against Satan was love and not punishment.

John 3:16 says, "For God loved the world in this way: He gave His One and Only Son, so that everyone who believes in Him will not perish but have eternal life." The weapons of forgiveness and love removed every obstacle sinful mankind had to turning back to the Father. The stronghold of sin was dismantled through God's love offering of His one and only Son, Jesus Christ. God's love covered the multitude of our sins.

Peter encouraged the suffering and persecuted believers in Asia Minor to love each other deeply, because love covers a multitude of sins (1 Peter 4:8). "Love covers a multitude of sins" simply means that love repeatedly forgives. We overcome hatred, injustice, or any wrongs done against us by demonstrating the power of love that comes from forgiveness. Satan uses hatred to stir up conflicts in churches, families, and nations, but we who have experienced the true love of God must counter him by using the weapons of forgiveness and love. When we understand the full power of God's forgiveness of our sins, we will learn to forgive others before they even ask us for forgiveness.

As human beings we have a tendency to forgive others only if they apologize or ask for forgiveness, or when we feel they have earned or deserve our forgiveness. However, that is not how true forgiveness, which brings restoration and healing, operates. We must be willing to forgive people, whether they ask for our forgiveness or not. Yes, if the offenders are humble enough, they will ask for forgiveness, but even if they don't ask for forgiveness, we are to forgive them. In doing this, we set ourselves free from the influence of the Devil.

God's forgiveness seems "backwards" in the sense that God forgives even before we, the offenders, ask Him for forgiveness (similarly, Romans 5:8 tells us Christ died for us while we were still sinners). To ask God to forgive us is to acknowledge our wrongs and open ourselves to the assuring power of the Holy Spirit to sanctify us and give us a new beginning. By confessing our sins before God or to each other, we are simply acknowledging that we are at fault and in need of a new beginning. First John 1:9 tells us, "If we confess our sins to him, he is faithful and just to forgive us our sins and to cleanse us from all wickedness" (NLT).

Satan engineered the fall of mankind into sin, but God used the weapon of forgiveness through the blood of Jesus to defeat Satan's plans. God sacrificed His own Son, Jesus Christ, to pay the price for sin and redeem us from the power of sin and death, while we were yet sinners. He did not say He would forgive us only if we showed signs of improvement. Rather, He demonstrated His love for us and provided forgiveness for our sins, even though our hearts were still far from Him. His love drew us closer into His presence. As we are going to see in this book, God expects the same from us—to love and forgive people just as He has loved and forgiven us.

God's Forgiveness Versus Human Forgiveness

When it comes to forgiving and loving like God does, we Christians have a long, long way to go. We sing songs about God's love and talk about forgiving others, but when it comes to actually loving and forgiving others, we are miles away from God's nature. We tend to love and forgive others only when we feel they deserve our love or have earned our forgiveness.

We forget that God forgave us because of His grace (unmerited or undeserved favor) and not because we earned our forgiveness.

One of the differences between God's forgiveness and man's forgiveness is that God's forgiveness is "within" our reach. It is already provided for all of our iniquities through the sacrifice of God's Son, Jesus Christ, way before we repent, and it is 100 percent assured, with no strings attached. Man's forgiveness, however, is "beyond" reach. A person must earn it, seek or ask for it, and sometimes beg for it. It is not assured, and sometimes when given, it comes with strings attached to it (i.e., don't offend me again).

With God's forgiveness, a person doesn't need to perform good deeds to earn his or her forgiveness. With human forgiveness, the offended person may decide whether to forgive or not forgive based on the magnitude of the offense or how he or she feels. With human forgiveness, a person needs to perform some good deeds in order to be considered a candidate for forgiveness. God forgives and never keeps records of wrongs, but people "forgive" and yet still keep a pile of records and memorize the wrongs done to them. God's forgiveness is not selective. It is unlimited and available to every sinner. But human forgiveness is limited, very selective, and available only to a few.

In this season we are living in, I strongly believe God wants to revive the church by first reviving us, His people, with the spirit of forgiveness, reconciliation, and love, both for each other and for the lost. As the people of God, we cannot claim we are under God's influence and yet hate each other and the people we are called to rescue from the power of sin and death. Furthermore, it is an injustice and a misrepresentation of the kingdom of God to even claim we are true children of God if the spirit of unforgiveness rules and reigns in our hearts. God's kingdom is rich in love, forgiveness, mercy, and grace, and like our God we should also be rich in love, forgiveness, mercy, and grace.

It is important to understand that forgiveness does not make you a weak person. Instead, it makes you strong and illustrates your deeper connection to God the Father. When you forgive, you win and the enemy loses, and you become a champion of peace and a minister of reconciliation. In addition, you will be called a blessed child of God

(Matthew 5:9). Only children of God are able to forgive and walk in peace because the living Spirit of God resides in their hearts. Their heart is full of God's riches of love, mercy, and forgiveness.

People who do not have the Holy Spirit residing in them or operating in their lives often struggle to love and forgive. We who have the indwelling power of the Holy Spirit, however, should not have such struggles. We should be quick to activate that forgiving Spirit of God in us and forgive those who have offended us. The Holy Spirit is there to empower us to do things we cannot do in our own strength, and forgiveness is one of those things we cannot do in our own strength.

If you have been in the church for a long time, you will probably agree that one of the things that is stopping the power of God from moving in the church and in the nations today is the spirit of unforgiveness. To be honest, the church is full of great and wonderful people, but many of these people have been hurt through words and things done to them to the point that their hearts have become saturated with anger, jealousy, bitterness, hatred, and unforgiveness. If we don't deal with these issues at a personal level, we will continue living in the same spiritual condition of powerless Christianity. Walking in peace begins with each one of us protecting our heart from corruptible things and choosing to forgive our enemies. Proverbs 4:23 warns us to guard our heart above all else, because out of it come the issues of life. If we don't learn to guard our heart from things such as bitterness, hatred, and anger, the spirit of unforgiveness will consume our lives, stall our spiritual growth, and cause us to destroy each other.

The frictions and divisions in the church have indeed put a limitation on what God can do through us and on what the church can accomplish among the nations. The question is, how can a divided "team" win a major championship? It is impossible. The same is true for the church today. Only through unity and teamwork can the church bring order to this disorganized and ungodly world we are living in today and be a light of peace, a light of hope, a source of life, and the foundation of nations.

In Mark 3:24–25 Jesus said these powerful words: "If a kingdom is divided against itself, that kingdom cannot stand" and "If a house is divided against itself, that house cannot stand." In context, Jesus was being accused by the scribes of driving out demons by the power of the ruler of demons (Beelzebul). But through His illustration, Jesus showed that *internal divisions* strengthen neither a kingdom nor a house. His power for casting out demons came from the kingdom of God and not from within the kingdom of darkness. Indeed, Satan cannot drive out Satan, He told them (Mark 3:23).

The lesson here is this: As long as we are divided or there is division among us, we cannot stand and powerfully advance the kingdom of God. That is why authentic forgiveness and repentance is such an important and powerful weapon in the kingdom of God. It mends the brokenhearted and restores and empowers us to leave the past behind us and team up in unity to forcefully advance God's kingdom. For the sake of the advancement of the kingdom of God, we need to forgive those who have offended and abused us and leave the past behind so that we can powerfully move in the anointing, glory, and presence of God and be "perfect" ambassadors of the great kingdom of God.

God is in the business of bringing emotional, physical, and inner healing to His people so that He can mightily use them for His kingdom. God is transforming His church back to its position as a house of healing, restoration, hope, and life. The enemy continues to try to corrupt and change the house of God into a house of pain, bad experiences, disappointments, and hatred, but the Bible declares that God's church shall forever stand and the forces of darkness shall not prevail against it (Matthew 16:18). Moreover, God also wants to restore relationships and unite His church, just as He is united as one with His Son and the Holy Spirit. Forgiveness is the vehicle of unity, peace, and restoration. There are just too many churches in the world today where people do not have a strong relationship with each other simply because of offense and unforgiveness. How can the church usher in the government of the kingdom of God with such disunity? I believe God is in the business of restoring the body of Christ, because the church is the voice of God, the voice of peace, the voice of reconciliation, and the foundation of stability in the world.

If the church is in fact the "foundation of stability" here on earth and yet we the church are unloving, hateful, and unforgiving, how can we be the light to the lost world in which we live? Forgiveness is the weapon we need to use if we are to change the unhealthy relationships we have in the church, in families, in marriages, and in the world.

Forgiveness is no weakness! It is a strength that gives you the ability and discipline to not allow unnecessary and unimportant things to take center stage in your heart. Besides, forgiveness can take you farther in life than you can even imagine. As you forgive others, you pave the way for God to act on your behalf to be your defender, your voice, your shield, and your protector and, above all, to use you as His instrument of love, unity, peace, and reconciliation.

It is through forgiveness we have received our new life from God, and it is by living a life of forgiveness that we demonstrate our appreciation for God's forgiveness of our sin. When we are hurt or offended, our fleshly nature demands vengeance, payback, and hatred, but the nature of God demands from us forgiveness, reconciliation, and love. That means we can successfully forgive people only when we are in Christ and walking in the fullness of His grace, mercy, and love.

When forgiveness is fully activated in the hearts of God's people, we are going to see revival and the fire of God breaking out. This is because our hearts will be full of God's purity and free of hatred, bitterness, and anger, and we will be worshiping our God in unity, joy, peace, and love as one. Our unforgiveness limits the work God wants to do through the church. God still works through people to demonstrate His power here on earth, but until our relationships with God and with each other are repaired, we are not going to see the full force of God's glory and power. And if we, the ones who are called by God's name and are to be channels through whom God works, are fighting each other or hating each other, it will be impossible for God to fully use us.

Forgiveness = Unity; Unity = God's Blessings

> *How good and pleasant it is when God's people live together in unity! It is like precious oil poured on the head, running down on the beard, running down on Aaron's beard, down on the collar*

> *of his robe. It is as if the dew of Hermon were falling on Mount Zion. For there the L*ORD *bestows his blessing, even life forevermore.* (Psalm 133:1–3 NIV)

Where there is forgiveness, there is unity; where there is unity, there are God's blessings; and where there are God's blessings, God's power and presence are evident. God's forgiveness of our sins has brought us into unity with Him and given us the blessings of being His children.

Before we move on to our next topic in the following chapter, here are a few scriptures to refresh our spirit and remind us of the great blessings that are upon us because of God's forgiveness of our sins.

- **The Blessing of Joy:** "How joyful is the one whose transgression is forgiven, whose sin is covered!" (Psalm 32:1).
- **The Blessing of Having Our Sins Covered by God:** "Blessed are those whose transgressions are forgiven, whose sins are covered" (Romans 4:7 NIV).
- **The Blessing of God Not Counting Our Past Sin against Us:** "Blessed is the one whose sin the Lord will never count against them" (Romans 4:8 NIV).
- **The Blessing of Forgiving Others:** "Forgive us our debts, as we also have forgiven our debtors" (Matthew 6:12).
- **The Blessing of Redemption:** "In whom we have redemption through his blood, even the forgiveness of sins" (Colossians 1:14 KJV).
- **The Blessing of Life:** "Then David said to Nathan, 'I have sinned against the L*ORD*.' Nathan replied, 'The L*ORD* has taken away your sin. You are not going to die'" (2 Samuel 12:13 NIV).

Chapter 2

THE MYSTERIOUS POWER OF FORGIVENESS

THERE IS GENUINE POWER IN FORGIVENESS. WHEN WE SAY THE WORDS "I FORGIVE YOU," people are indeed forgiven and released. Yet this concept is difficult, if not impossible, for the "natural mind" to grasp. The power of forgiveness is fueled by the power of the Holy Spirit, backed by the government of God, and released by the word of our mouths (tongues). Thus, there is power in our tongues, or words. What we say and how we say it has the power to affect a person in a positive or a negative way. In fact, our words have the power to release a person from the influence of the Devil or keep that person under the Evil One's influence. In this chapter we will look closely at the "mystery" power of forgiveness, and in our next chapter at the power of the tongue. Forgiveness takes place when we declare to a person with our mouth, "I forgive you." We can't forgive silently or just inside our heart. We need to declare it and speak it. When we do, that person will be forgiven.

You Have the Authority and Power to Forgive Sinners

As Jesus was commissioning His disciples in John 20:21–23, He said to them, "Peace to you! As the Father has sent Me, I also send you." After saying this, He breathed on them and said, "Receive the Holy Spirit. If you forgive the sins of any, they are forgiven them; if you retain the sins of any, they are retained." It is important to understand that the power we possess to forgive the sins of a person comes from Jesus Himself. Jesus not only had the power to heal the sick but He also had the power to forgive the sins of people. Throughout His ministry, He demonstrated the power of forgiveness. When He forgave the sins of a paralytic in Mark 2:5–7, the people who heard Him, including the scribes (Jewish writers or professional theologians), were astounded and accused Him of blaspheming. They said, "Who can forgive sin but God alone?" These people could not believe that Jesus had the power and authority to forgive sin. This was a mystery to them.

Yet Jesus not only claimed the power to forgive sin but also said to His disciples, "If you forgive the sins of any, they are forgiven them; if you retain the sins of any, they are retained." First, this is a confirmation of Jesus' power and authority to forgive sin: What He opens, no one can close; what He closes, no one can open. He was now assigning the same authority and power to His disciples. Just like Jesus, their Master, the disciples would be able to forgive the sins of any, and they would, in fact, be forgiven; or they could "retain" the sins of any, and their sins would be retained. They now had the keys to the kingdom so that whatever they bound on earth would be bound in heaven, and whatever they loosed on earth would be loosed in heaven. As disciples of Jesus Christ, we have the power and authority to forgive. What God alone does (forgive sin), He has empowered us to do on His behalf: Forgive those who trespass against us.

Every time you forgive the sins of others, you are representing the kingdom of God, and, I'm sorry to say, each time you don't forgive someone, you are representing the kingdom of darkness. It is in you to forgive! It is important to understand, in context, the depth of Jesus' commission to His disciples in John 20:21–23. First, the disciples were afraid of the Jews (Jerusalem authorities) and could not talk publicly about Jesus (John 7:13). And in John 20:19, we are told that because of their fear of the Jews (probably fear of persecution), the disciples had gathered together with doors locked. Notice the first words the resurrected Jesus said to His disciples when He suddenly appeared to them: "Peace to you." He said this to them twice and then said, "As the Father has sent Me, I also send you." The first question we need to ask before we go further is this: What did God the Father send Jesus to do that His disciples were to continue to do? Jesus' words in Luke 4:18, quoting Isaiah 61:1, can help us answer that question:

> *"The Spirit of the Lord is on Me, because He has anointed Me to preach good news to the poor. He has sent Me to proclaim freedom to the captives and recovery of sight to the blind, to set free the oppressed."*

The highlight, or focal point, of Jesus' mission was to proclaim freedom to the captives and to set free the oppressed. Jesus' disciples were to continue with the great mission of God to set the oppressed and captives free through the power of the Holy Spirit. Jesus bestowed upon His disciples the authority and power to forgive people of their sins or to retain their sins. In other words, the disciples had the power either to open the doors of the kingdom of darkness and free the captives (sinners) from the bondage of sin and death by forgiving them or to keep those who rejected the good news of the kingdom in the prison of sin and death by not forgiving them.

Notice that Jesus did not instruct His disciples to perform any special ceremony before forgiving the sins of people. All the disciples needed was the Holy Spirit, whom the Lord had breathed on them, and they could declare, "You are forgiven." This gives us an idea of why the Devil fights people tooth and nail to keep them from proclaiming, "I forgive you" or "We forgive." He understands the power behind those words to set people free from his control and manipulation. Consequently, Satan seeks to magnify the offense and the pain caused by it so that we do not forgive the person who offends us and as a result, that person remains in his custody and we are trapped in our anger, bitterness, and hatred.

The power of forgiveness works like a mystery. With our natural eyes, we cannot see the great work it does in both the heart of a person who forgives and the one who is forgiven. Its power and impact upon a person's life is difficult to explain or understand. This is because forgiveness is a spiritual weapon designed by God to release people from the influence, control, and power of the kingdom of darkness brought about by the sin of Adam and Eve. When we forgive someone, a shift occurs in the spiritual realm, just as there was a shift when God forgave our many sins. When God forgave us, we moved from being children of darkness (Satan), mastered by the power of sin and sentenced to hell, to being children of the light (God), mastered by the power of the Holy Spirit and given eternal life. Our act of forgiveness has the power to change a person's direction in life. God has given us that power to free people so that they will be freed from the hands of the enemy. Forgiveness is a secret weapon God has given to us. We are to use this powerful weapon against Satan by forgiving those he has bound and setting them free. Don't let bitterness, anger, and offense come between you and God's mission and purpose for your life. Forgive, forgive, and keep forgiving, and let God be your defender against those who offend you.

Don't Let Anger Lead You to Unrighteous Acts

Paul wrote, "Be angry and do not sin. Don't let the sun go down on your anger, and don't give the Devil an opportunity" (Ephesians 4:26–27). Notice Paul did not say, "Don't be angry at all." Rather, he was saying, "Be angry; however, don't let your anger lead you to unrighteous acts." We must understand that offense and unrestrained anger is a trap from the Devil to get us off course in our walk with God, a subject we will discuss in greater detail in chapter 4. Paul's point is that while anger is at times justified, we must be careful not to let anger consume our heart and lead us to act or react in ungodly ways. When anger knocks on your door, always turn your heart to the Word of God and to the Holy Spirit to comfort and empower you to withstand the testing of your faith. The Holy Spirit will comfort and enable you to forgive the one who has offended you so that you may live at peace and in peace with that person.

Romans 12:21 warns us, "Do not be conquered by evil, but conquer evil with good." In life, we will suffer hatred, injustice, offense, and even persecution. Our response to such things is critical. A worldly, or "carnal," person responds to hatred with retaliation, but a spiritual, or Holy Spirit-influenced person, responds with God's grace. This does not mean we just overlook what has been done against us, but instead we understand that the offense is the Devil's weapon, designed to trap us into evil actions. We should respond to hatred, offense, or persecution with God's weapon of forgiveness. God, in His Son, Jesus Christ, conquered evil (sin) on the cross with the goodness, or weapon, of forgiveness.

Today we are who we are in Christ because of God's grace and mercy. We are not to let evil conquer us but instead conquer evil with the goodness of our God; that is, with love, mercy, grace, and forgiveness. To keep anger from leading us into unrighteous acts and thus conquering us, we need to live in the Spirit and not in the flesh, or according to the old sinful nature. The reason some "Christians" respond to circumstances in ungodly ways is because of the dominion of the flesh in their lives. Yes, the pain of being hurt greatly tempts us to respond in kind, but we must not give in to the flesh. The Bible tells us to live in the Spirit and not in the flesh so that we do not fulfill the desires of our flesh. The flesh leads to overreaction, revenge, hatred, bitterness, anger, and unforgiveness, but the Spirit leads to grace, mercy, forgiveness, and victory over the tactics of the Devil.

As a son or daughter of God, it is crucial to understand that anger can corrupt the spirit of God in you. The only anger you should have is a "holy anger" toward unrighteousness and injustice because you serve a God of righteousness and justice. Holy anger comes from the depth of your love for God and for His people. To do anything in bitterness and without love helps nobody. In fact, it brings harm rather than good. Do things in the perfect love of God, and you will build up people and motivate them to do what is right. Shouting, screaming, or responding in kind does not effectively change a tense situation, but instead escalates it and may lead to isolation of the parties involved. Do things out of love and not out of bitterness or anger.

Following in the Footsteps of the Master

Throughout His ministry here on earth, Jesus used the power of His words (tongue) to forgive, to heal, to cast out demons, and to reconnect people to God. For example, in Luke 7:48 He said to a sinful woman (probably a prostitute), "Your sins are forgiven." And in Mark 2:5, when Jesus saw the faith of the four friends of a paralytic, He said to the man, "Son, your sins are forgiven."

On both occasions we see Jesus use the power of the spoken word (tongue) to declare freedom or forgiveness. The people who were around Him were amazed because, according to them, only God had the power to forgive sin. The power to forgive the sins of people is now available to believers in Christ, but unfortunately it is seldom used.

You have the power to speak words of forgiveness, healing, and freedom to people so that they will indeed be set free. However, if you choose to use your tongue wrongly by cursing or speaking evil words against others or even yourself, you need to understand this: What you declare with your mouth may come to pass because there is power in your tongue to establish what you speak. The words you speak are powerful (Matthew 16:19) and can either build up or destroy a person. We are to follow in the footsteps of Jesus Christ our Master by speaking words of freedom, peace, healing, love, and salvation and not words of bondage.

If there is one thing we all need to work on if we are to effectively follow in the footsteps of Jesus, it is how we use our tongue. The Bible tells us to avoid worthless, irreverent, and empty speech or discussions because they lead us only to a greater measure of godlessness and are unprofitable to our spiritual growth and that of others. We cannot use the weapon of forgiveness effectively without taming our tongue from speaking evil and letting the living Word of God flow from our mouth.

Declaring Forgiveness

By declaring with your mouth, "I forgive," you are releasing yourself from the power or influence of anger, bitterness, hatred, and unforgiveness. Forgiveness has the power to calm down a broken, upset, and bitter heart, restore love for one another, and consequently build a strong community of believers and world changers. When you understand the power of forgiveness, you discover a weapon that neither Satan nor all his armies can withstand. Moreover, you are going to avoid his trap and overcome the stumbling block of offense. Satan wants you to be offended so that he can weaken you, isolate you, accuse you before God, and defeat you. He wants the offense to hurt and become the focus of your mind and heart.

We all struggle in one way or another with forgiveness, not because we are incapable of forgiveness, but because of the pain of offense. Yet unforgiveness hinders us from walking with God in His presence and glory. Furthermore, unforgiveness is a hindrance to worship, while forgiveness is the doorway to acceptable worship of God (Matthew 5:23–24). Forgiveness can lead you to greater things in God and give you a clear vision of God's calling upon your life by taking your mind and heart away from the pain of offense and directing them to the heart and passion of God.

Forgiveness Can Bring a Breakthrough in Your Life

Very few people know the depth and power of forgiveness. Forgiveness is not just an act of kindness toward an offender or enemy. It is a key to a breakthrough in your relationship with God. Unforgiveness, on the other hand, not only can hinder your breakthrough in life but also can hinder your prayers from being answered.

In Matthew 5:23–24 Jesus said, "If you are offering your gift on the altar, and there you remember that your brother has something against you, leave your gift there in front of the altar. First go and be reconciled with your brother, and then come and offer your gift."

These are very important verses because they reveal how we should approach God when we come into His presence in worship. We are to come with a spirit of forgiveness and reconciliation. Matthew 5:23–24 presents a pathway to God's answering our prayers. Often we do not see our prayers answered because we approach God dutifully and religiously, yet we have offended people or our heart is full of bitterness over being offended. Jesus makes it clear that God cares very much how we treat one another. Therefore, before we approach God or make our requests known to Him, we must make sure we reconcile with people who have something against us and forgive those we have something against. With such a spirit, God will accept our worship, answer our requests, and open the windows of heaven for us.

When you forgive, what matters even more than the act of forgiveness is the spirit behind your forgiveness, because the spirit behind forgiveness has the power to avoid the traps and break the chains of the Devil. The Devil's goal is to develop the spirit of unforgiveness in you so that you are blinded to the plans of God for your life. When you are focused on your pain, hurts, and disappointments, it is very difficult to hear the voice of God or see the direction God wants to lead you in because your heart is callused with bitterness, anger, hatred, and resentment.

Most people forgive for the sake of forgiving or because someone told them to forgive. Such a shallow approach to forgiving people explains why so many struggle to let go of the pain of offense. You need to forgive. First, you need to forgive, not because someone told you to, but because God has forgiven your many sins. Second, you need to forgive because forgiveness is a weapon that destroys the Devil's plans to cause unrest in the body of God and damage relationships in marriages and families. Whenever you feel like you are struggling to forgive and let go of the pain of offense in your heart, remember the following:

- God has forgiven you your many sins, so you have no reason to withhold forgiveness from others (Matthew 6:12; John 3:16–17).
- You are in God, and in God there is forgiveness (Psalm 130:4).
- If you don't forgive others, God won't forgive you (Matthew 6:14–15; Mark 11:25).
- You have experienced God's mercy so that you can demonstrate God's mercy to others (Titus 3:5).
- You are an ambassador of God's kingdom, representing God's interests here on earth, and one of those interests is forgiving people.
- You are called to follow in the footsteps of your Master, Jesus Christ. Jesus forgave sinners everywhere He went, so you too must forgive and carry forgiveness everywhere you go.

When You Forgive, God Illuminates Your Vision and Calling

To illustrate another aspect of the mystery power of forgiveness, let me briefly share my own experience of how forgiveness gave me a breakthrough in my life and illuminated God's vision, passion, and mission and calling for my life. When I first gave my life to the Lord and made a commitment to live for and serve Him, I went through a turbulent and stormy experience I never expected. The storm for me involved experiencing prejudice, hatred, rejection, manipulation, injustice, and slander. To my surprise, these things did not come from "ungodly" people but from "godly" people—people I looked up to for inspiration and encouragement to live for God, people I respected, deeply honored, and truly loved.

I thought opposition came only from enemies, but I was wrong. Through it all, I discovered that the Devil more often uses people of influence in the community of believers to discourage the young and upcoming generation of leaders from taking over someday and continuing with the advancement of the kingdom of God. Consequently, the young, passionate, aspiring leaders are opposed, intimidated, rebuked, and manipulated instead of being trained, supported, guided, and encouraged to serve God. I was heartbroken and discouraged. I contemplated giving up ministry and moving on to other things, but the Holy Spirit convicted me deeply of my disappointments, bitterness, and anger, and showed me that my real enemy was not the people opposing me but Satan, who was trying to kill the call of God upon my life.

Before you take things personally and lose your temper and sense of peace, inquire of the Lord about why you are going through what you are going through. The Lord, who does not test or tempt us with evil (James 1:13), will show you exactly who is fighting you and why he is fighting you. When you discover who is fighting you and why, you will not turn against people but against the real enemy, the Devil, who constantly fights God's purpose and will for God's people. Don't be surprised when good people you respect, look up to, and honor offend you or let you down, but don't turn against them or take the battle to them. Turn to God in prayer and intercession. Remember that people are not your real enemy; Satan simply hides behind people so that he can use them to stop you from doing the will of God.

Satan will always try to influence the character, behavior, and actions of people so that he can incite hatred and stir up confusion and disunity in the body of Christ. Knowing who the real enemy is can help you focus on God and on His vision for your life instead of focusing on people. When you are treated unfairly, never let anger corrupt your spirit or consume your heart. Instead, turn to God through the weapons of forgiveness, prayer, praise, and worship, and the Lord will fight the battle on your behalf and give you victory. When I was experiencing opposition in my life, I turned to the Lord in prayer, and the first words the Lord whispered to me were, "Forgive. Don't focus on people, but focus on Me. It is not people fighting you, but the enemy trying to work through people to distract and stop you from doing the work I have called you to do."

The Lord continued and said, "Be humble. Do not retaliate or do things to prove people wrong, but stand on My Word and do what My Word says, and I will give you a breakthrough and use you as an instrument of inspiration and to win lost souls for My kingdom." These words transformed my attitude and character and the way I respond today to offense or problems in my life. I immediately forgave the people who had opposed and offended me, and the Lord lifted the weight of unforgiveness from my life. Thus, my vision and the call of God upon my life were illuminated, and my zeal and passion for God was reenergized. It was like I was reborn again. My mind was renewed, and my heart was cleansed from the bitterness and hurt, and God put His Word and His Spirit in my heart. I stopped focusing on people and on the wrongs that had been done against me, and I started focusing on God and what He wanted to do through me.

Through forgiveness, I received deliverance, and I have not been the same since. Hatred, anger, unforgiveness, and bitterness have no power over me because the Holy Spirit has destroyed their stronghold. I am free to live a new life in Christ, minister from a pure heart and clear mind, and love people without strings attached. This is why I write this book with urgency to all in the body of Christ. Forgiveness is a powerful weapon that can bring revival and revolutionize the church. Forgiveness is a mystery power of God that destroys all the tactics of the Devil and makes a way for our breakthrough in life. I pray you will soften your heart to the Word of God and forgive everyone who has offended, abused, and mistreated you. Now is your time to experience a new and fresh beginning in the Lord and have your heart cleansed from all the hurts, bitterness, and anger so you can walk in the power of God. This does not mean you will not experience offense, but you will be ready to take it on with the weapons of forgiveness, prayer, praise, and worship.

Life is full of offense or problems, but the problems, trials, and tests in life are there to take you up to the next level. There is no victory without a battle. Furthermore, some challenges are there to test your foundation and the stability of your faith in God, your spiritual maturity, and your readiness to go to the next level in life. Many people falter in the face of challenges or trials and do not respond in a godly way to them. If we all looked at trials or challenges as opportunities to grow spiritually and responded in the strength and power of God's Word, we would be a force to be reckoned with, and Satan would be defeated.

The Call of God Is Not for the Easily Offended

When God called Jeremiah to urge the people of Judah (the southern kingdom) to turn away from their sins and back to God, the prophet was thrown into prison (Jeremiah 37) and then into a cistern (Jeremiah 38). He was rejected by his neighbors, family, false priests, friends, kings, and fellow citizens (Jeremiah 11:19–21; 12:6; 20:1–2; 28:1–17; 26:8; 36:23). Jeremiah's life was extremely difficult, despite his love for and obedience to God. When he complained to God about his experience, God basically said, "If you think this is bad, how are you going to cope when it gets really tough?" (cf. Jeremiah 12:5). The call of God is not for the easily offended or weak-hearted; it is for those who totally surrender their lives and comfort to the leadership of God. The life of a Christian is not an easy one. It is one battle after another, and we must win those battles if we are to progress in our spiritual lives.

Living for God requires perseverance, endurance, humility, and a forgiving and loving heart. Jeremiah persevered and endured persecution. His humility, forgiveness, and loving heart for the people of Judah was demonstrated when he repeatedly went back to preach to the same people who had persecuted him. In the eyes of the world, Jeremiah was not a successful prophet of God, for nobody listened to him or followed him. But in God's eyes Jeremiah was a very successful man of God because he obeyed and followed the word of God. Success in God's eyes is measured by our faith and obedience to His Word. Regardless of opposition, rejection, and personal cost, we must courageously and faithfully follow after God.

Jeremiah's rejection is a great picture of Jesus, our Messiah, who was also rejected by the people He came to save. And because of His rejection, His followers also can expect to be rejected by the world. You may have been rejected by your friends or family for pursuing God, but don't take that personally. Rather, live each day to demonstrate the true character and nature of God in everything you do and say. Let people see God in action in you through your love and mercy.

Jesus said, "You will be hated by everyone because of My name. But the one who endures to the end will be delivered" (Mathew 10:22). And in Luke 6:22, He said, "You are blessed when people hate you, when they exclude you, insult you, and slander your name as evil because of the Son of Man." And finally in John 15:18–19, He said, "If the world hates you, understand that it hated Me before it hated you. If you were of the world, the world would love you as its own. However, because you are not of the world, but I have chosen you out of it, the world hates you."

It is amazing to see that when you do things according to the world or behave like the world, very few people will oppose you or even care what you are doing, but the moment you begin to pursue God wholeheartedly and do things for God and in His way, you will be opposed and attacked like no one's business, even by the most "religious" people. Why? It is because when you do the will of God and walk in His Word, the Devil is threatened to his core, and he will do anything to stop you, including using some familiar faces.

As Paul said in Ephesians 6:12, your battle is not against flesh and blood (human opponents) but against spiritual forces of darkness (Satan and his agents). Don't go after people or try to prove them wrong. Instead, fix your eyes on Christ, and forgive your offenders quickly so that you can maintain a pure heart before Yahweh's holy name and walk in the supernatural power of the kingdom of God through practicing love, justice, and mercy toward those around you.

The Bible tells us to count ourselves "dead to sin but alive to God in Christ Jesus" (Romans 6:11). One of the best ways to react to offense is to play "dead." Simply forgive and hold no grudge toward anyone so that you may live in peace and focus on what God has called you to do. When you discover this truth, you will also recover your vision, dream, and purpose in life. In this world you will be offended. It is important to know who your real enemy is so that you do not become a victim, but rather a victor in Christ. God wants to use you and revive His will and purpose for your life, but unforgiveness will hold Him back from doing so. Forgive and you will rescue your life from the Devil's influence. Don't let negative words people have spoken against you or bad things that have happened to you produce seeds of bitterness, anger, and hate in your heart.

Guard your heart from anything and everything that desires to corrupt the Spirit of God in you, and pay more attention to what God wants to do through you than to the corrupt words of others. Don't spend your life trying to defend yourself, or to justify yourself, or to prove your offenders wrong. Instead, get on your knees and use the weapons of forgiveness and prayer, and watch God fight for you (cf. Exodus 14:14), bless you, and enlarge your territories. The God who has called you is bigger, greater, and more powerful than the enemy seeking to destroy you. Trust in Him and lean not on your understanding when you are going through trials, and He will direct your path and make a way for you (cf. Proverbs 3:5–6). Don't give the enemy an opportunity to influence you. Resist him by forgiving your offenders, and he will flee from you (cf. James 4:7).

In the next chapter, we will look at the power of the tongue. But let us here briefly note how the tongue relates to the mystery power of forgiveness. Simply with your tongue you can alter some things or situations in your life and in the lives of others. God has given you the power to declare things to be established according to God's grace and will. Your tongue is crucial and extremely important. If you can control your tongue from speaking worthless words, you can surely control your life and future so that you will live to see God's promises over your life fully fulfilled. Forgiveness works like a mystery simply because of the power of the tongue.

James 3:2 says this about the power of the tongue: "Indeed, we all make many mistakes. For if we could control our tongues, we would be perfect and could also control ourselves in every other way" (NLT).

Most of the time what makes us stumble or causes others to stumble in their walk with God are words that proceed from the mouth. If we could control our tongue, we could rescue our lives and the lives of many others from the influences of the kingdom of darkness. The words we speak are powerful and can affect a person in a positive or a negative way. Consequently, many people have been led astray by the ungodly words of those who claim to be believers in Christ but lack Christ's heart and God's Spirit.

In James 1:26, James wrote, "If you claim to be religious but don't control your tongue, you are fooling yourself, and your religion is worthless" (NLT). If we claim to be children of God, we must demonstrate it through the words we speak and the things we do. Our actions speak, but so do our words, and they have the power to produce either spiritual life or spiritual death. When we speak words of life that build up and empower others, our religion is worthwhile and, in fact, will change the world and bring real revival.

Controlling your tongue is crucial if you are to win spiritual battles in life, walk in revival, and demonstrate the compassionate heart of Jesus Christ. Your tongue has the power to bring you a breakthrough in life and move your life toward the power and presence of God. It has the power to bring you victory; yet at the same time, if it is not properly used, it has the power to bring destruction.

Forgiveness is declared and established through the power of the tongue. That is why forgiveness is a mysterious power. It takes only a person to speak it, and it is established. In order for us to walk in the power of forgiveness, we need to learn how to control our tongue and use it for the purpose of advancing the kingdom of God. If we don't know how to control our tongue or use it, our careless words will make other people stumble. Proverbs 15:2 says, "The tongue of the wise makes knowledge acceptable, but the mouth of fools spouts folly" (NASB). How you use your tongue can either bring souls into the kingdom of God or block them from the kingdom. What you say reflects who you are, whose you are, and who influences you. Your words tell a lot about you.

Chapter 3
THE POWER OF YOUR TONGUE

Change What You Say and You Will Be an Overcomer

THE TONGUE IS ONE OF THE SMALLEST PARTS OF THE BODY, YET IT IS EXTREMELY POWERFUL, and it is venomous if it is not used properly. As small as it is, it has caused many great men and women of God to fall and lose credibility. It has also caused many others of both higher and lower ranks in society to fall, destroying families, friendships, marriages, churches, and even nations. The tongue has quenched many moves of God in the history of the church and hindered many Christians from experiencing the presence and fire of God. On the other hand, the tongue also has been a powerful instrument for proclaiming to the nations the life-changing oracles of God. God established the earth, the sea, and everything that is within them through the power of the spoken word (Psalm 33:6, 9; Genesis 1:3). To this day, things are declared, decreed, and established, whether good or bad, through the spoken word.

Many people's lives today are in shambles as a result of words spoken into their lives by their parents, spiritual guardians, or other people of influence in their lives. To reverse those negative and ungodly words spoken over your life, you first need to use the weapon of forgiveness and then the weapon and power of the spoken word of God to override everything said against you that is contrary to what God says about you. It is important to understand that every evil word spoken against your life has the power to affect your future. Evil words have the power to bring destruction because they are backed by the power of the kingdom of darkness.

Many people ignore or forget how powerful the words we speak can be. Words spoken with the intent to hurt, demoralize, injure, or stir up confusion do exactly those things, because the tongue is powerful and destructive. The question is, how can something so tiny be so powerful?

In this chapter we will look at the power of the tongue and discover why Satan takes such pleasure in influencing people to use their tongue to speak evil, proclaim curses, and offend people. Additionally, we will discover the power of the spoken word of God. Just one word from God can change the atmosphere, build up a community of believers, and destroy the kingdom of darkness. As children of God, we have the power in our tongues to forgive people's sins, to bring freedom, to mend the brokenhearted, to give life to the lifeless, to heal, and to proclaim liberty to the captives. The Bible talks a lot about the power of the tongue, so it is important for us to look at this topic in depth and learn how we can use our tongue to advance the kingdom of God and set the captives free.

We Overcome Evil through the Spoken Word of God

God's children overcome, triumph, conquer, and defeat the enemy by the blood of the Lamb (Jesus Christ) and by the "word" of our testimony (cf. Revelation 12:11). In other words, we defeat Satan and his agents by "speaking" the word of God. Jesus, our Master, demonstrated the power of the tongue, or spoken word, many times in His ministry. On many occasions He merely spoke the word and the sick were healed, sinners were forgiven, and the dead were brought back to life. But in Matthew 21:18–22 Jesus used the power of the "tongue" to demonstrate to His disciples how powerful a "word spoken in faith" can be in bringing forth the desired results. Let's turn to Matthew 21:18–22, and see Jesus' illustration of the power of the tongue.

> *Early in the morning, as He was returning to the city, He was hungry. Seeing a lone fig tree by the road, He went up to it and found nothing on it except leaves. And He said to it, "May no fruit ever come from you again!" At once the fig tree withered. When the disciples saw it, they were amazed and said, "How did the fig tree wither so quickly?" Jesus answered them, "I assure you: If you have*

faith and do not doubt, you will not only do what was done to the fig tree, but even if you tell [speak to] this mountain, 'Be lifted up and thrown into the sea,' it will be done. And if you believe, you will receive whatever you ask [speak] for in prayer."

Jesus' cursing of the fig tree was not a thoughtless or angry act of getting back at the fig tree for not producing fruit. Rather, it was a demonstration of His unhappiness at religion without substance. The fig tree looked good from a distance but on closer examination was found to be fruitless. The religious leaders of Jesus' day looked very spiritual outwardly, but inwardly they had no godly substance (fruit). But beyond this, Matthew 21:18–22 shows us something very deep, powerful, and important. It shows us the power of the tongue, or the spoken word. Jesus "said," or "spoke," to the fig tree, "May no fruit ever come from you again," and at once the fig tree withered, much to the surprise and amazement of Jesus' disciples. What is also interesting here is that Jesus told His disciples that if they too had faith and did not doubt, they could speak (use the power of the spoken word) to the mountains, "Be lifted up and thrown into the sea," and it would be done.

Words spoken in good or bad faith can produce good or bad fruit accordingly; such is the power of the spoken word. That is why it is so important to put your tongue under the Holy Spirit's control. The "tongue" has the power to direct a person's life in the right or wrong direction; it has the ability to bring life or death. As we have already stated, many people's lives today are as a result of words spoken over their lives—either by themselves, or by their parents, or by someone else. What you say about yourself or your children is what you or they eventually become. Likewise, what you allow others to say about you, your future, your marriage, and your family is what you will become, because words are that powerful.

This explains why many people today are chasing after "prophetic words for their lives" from prophets. People travel great distances just to get a prophetic word because they believe words spoken over them by a prophet will truly come to pass. I am who I am today because God used men and women of God to speak His word over my life, declaring that one day I would serve the Lord. Today I am doing exactly what was spoken over my life many years ago. But, sadly, many people have been led astray in their walk with God because someone "prophesied" or said to them that they were going to get rich, and as a result they started chasing after riches instead of chasing after God. Words are very powerful. They have the ability to shape and direct a person's future and spiritual life. This is why Satan uses hate speech to divide, conquer, and destroy people.

Examine every word spoken over your life to see if it is really coming from the Spirit of God and lines up with the Word of God. One way to tell that the word spoken over you is not from God is that it leads you away from the presence of God, causes you to stumble in your faith, fellowship, relationship, and walk with God, brings division, or does not contribute to your hunger and thirst for righteousness. No word from the mouth of God can lead a person to a sinful lifestyle or to death. God is a life-giver. Every word from Him brings life, courage, motivation, edification, and guidance and gives insight and instructions on how to live powerfully for Him and be His chosen people, holy and righteous.

Do not believe every spirit, but test the spirits to determine if they are from God, because many false prophets have gone out into the world. (1 John 4:1)

First John 4:1 tells us not to believe everyone who claims to speak by the Spirit but to test him or her first to see if the spirit that person is speaking from comes from God. In other words, we must first check to see if the person's words match what God says in the Bible, promote a godly lifestyle, and lead to spiritual growth and devotion to Christ. If we are not careful, words spoken by a so-called "man of God" (or "woman of God") can lead us away from God and into the kingdom of darkness. The world today is full of people who claim to speak on God's behalf and yet lead many away from His presence. For example, I know of one minister who told his congregation to eat grass because he claimed God gave him this message, and the people actually believed him, acted on his word, and ate grass.

There are many documented incidents of so-called "men of God" or "prophets" who have asked their congregants to do things that are totally unholy and unbiblical, and the people, acting on the spoken word of man, went ahead and did exactly what they were told. The end result in most cases was ungodly and sometimes deadly. This shows again how powerful the tongue, or spoken word, can really be. Anything spoken that does not lead you to love God more, increase your passion for His Word, and live a holy life is not worthy of your ears, time, money, dedication, and attention. What you give your ear to is what goes into your heart and, consequently, is what you become.

The evil words people speak divulge the true nature and content of their heart. In Luke 6:45 Jesus said that evil speech and deeds overflow from the evil stored up in one's heart. Now imagine if you stored up only the Word of God in your heart. You would speak to motivate, encourage, help, and edify people rather than to bring them down. Proverbs 12:18 says, "The tongue of the wise brings healing." Your tongue must be used to speak words that bring healing and restoration to people and not the other way around. Don't let Satan use you through the words you speak, but instead submit your tongue to the influence of the Holy Spirit, so that the Lord can use you to speak and communicate His word. Before you speak anything, remember that for every careless word you speak, you will be required by God to give an account on the day of judgment (Matthew 12:36–37).

A Small and Yet Deadly Weapon—the Tongue

> *So too, though the tongue is a small part of the body, it boasts great things. Consider how large a forest a small fire ignites. And the tongue is a fire. The tongue, a world of unrighteousness, is placed among the parts of our bodies. It pollutes the whole body, sets the course of life on fire, and is set on fire by hell. Every sea creature, reptile, bird, or animal is tamed and has been tamed by man, but no man can tame the tongue. It is a restless evil, full of deadly poison. We praise our Lord and Father with it, and we curse men who are made in God's likeness with it.* (James 3:5–9)

The tongue, as we have already stated, is a tiny part of the body, and yet it is one of the most powerful and influential parts of the human body. Just as a pilot or captain guides a very large ship through fierce winds, the tongue has the power to direct a person's life in the midst of the storm. When you are experiencing a storm in your life, the words you speak and confess are crucial because they can either plunge your life deeper into the storm or take you out of the storm. James compares the damage and devastation the tongue can do to that of a raging fire that starts from a small spark but quickly sets a great forest on fire. Whether you use your tongue to proclaim a blessing of God or a curse, it surely will produce the intended results. Satan uses the tongue as a weapon to divide people and pit them against one another. Clearly, he has done a great job of that because if you look around the world today, you find that division, hatred, and anger are on the increase and out of control. An uncontrolled tongue can do terrible damage to the body and family of God. Its destruction spreads quickly, because it is difficult to stop or control.

Proverbs 10:19 tells us, "When there are many words, sin is unavoidable, but the one who controls his lips is wise." Before you speak anything, ponder your words, because if they are spoken in hatred or anger, they can bring destruction. Ask yourself this question: Is my speech prudent and productive? If you don't know what to say, King Solomon, that great and wise man, has some good advice in Proverbs 10:19: "Keep your mouth shut" (NLT).

As Christians, we are to use our tongue as a weapon of God against Satan and his agents. We are to speak words that build up, mend the brokenhearted, and bring forth life. "The lips of the righteous know what is appropriate, but the mouth of the wicked, only what is perverse" (Proverbs 10:32). As righteous persons whose hearts have been redeemed by Christ, we know what God requires of us: to bless and not to curse.

The words we speak as Christians call for a response in the spiritual realm. In today's society, it is often deemed acceptable to tear other people down verbally through gossip and backbiting. It is unfortunate that this spirit has now entered into the body of Christ, consequently bringing the spiritual growth of God's people to a standstill and giving non-Christians the opportunity to label us as hypocrites because we gossip, slander, and use ungodly words, just as the world does.

In Galatians 5:15, the apostle Paul said, "But if you bite and devour one another, watch out, or you will be consumed by one another." Be careful with words you speak. They can hurt other people and bring dissension, and dissension leads to ungodly reactions, attitudes, and behaviors. Before you speak, think about the impact your words will have upon those around you.

Apology Accepted—But the Damage Is Already Done

It is sad to say that most of us think that if we curse a person, we can just apologize and that ends the story. Unfortunately, the story doesn't end there, because evil words spoken can never be reversed simply by making an apology. This is because every evil word spoken calls for a response in the spiritual realm. If a mother or father says to a child, "You will never amount to anything in life," a later apology is certainly appropriate. However, parents need to understand that what they have decreed and declared over their son or daughter has been established. It takes prayers and intercession, not an apology, to reverse a curse. An apology is good because it helps to restore the relationship between people, but it doesn't reverse the fulfillment of the words spoken. The apology may be accepted, but the damage has already been done and has gone forth like a fire in the forest.

If we truly want to change the world with the power of the gospel, we need to allow the Holy Spirit to melt our hearts, cleanse us, transform us, and deposit His words into our hearts so that we can speak as godly, chosen, anointed kingdom people. It is a joke to claim we are a kingdom people if the words we speak are totally of the world. How do we use the same mouth both to praise our Lord and Father and to curse people, who are made in God's likeness (James 3:9)? Kingdom people know how to use their tongue—against Satan and not against God's own people. They think before they speak, they know how to control their tongue, they don't talk out of bitterness or anger but out of love, and they always remember that words are like a fire that can spread quickly out of control.

In our own strength, we cannot tame our tongue, but the Holy Spirit can help us tame it and give us words to speak. He can give you the ability to control your tongue when you are under pressure or when offense comes. And controlling your tongue when you are offended or angered demonstrates the character of Christ and the wisdom of God in you. The secret is this: "Be quick to listen, slow to speak and slow to become angry" (James 1:19 NIV). Always be gentle and humble when you are experiencing injustice, and don't let your ego spoil a great opportunity to showcase God's character.

Your Words Reveal What Is Hidden in Your Heart

Matthew 12:34 records these words of Jesus: "Brood of vipers! How can you speak good things when you are evil? For the mouth speaks from the overflow of the heart." Here Jesus was reminding the religious leaders of His day that "their evil words" flowed from the abundance of evil that was stored within their hearts. The words we speak reveal what is hidden within our hearts because our words and thoughts are deeply and intimately connected to the heart. Our words disclose who we really are. We use the same mouth to speak for God (blessings) and to speak on the Devil's behalf (cursing). But the truth is, we are either an advocate of evil or an advocate of good, and we can't be both. James 3:10–12 says this:

> *Praising and cursing come out of the same mouth. My brothers, these things should not be this way. Does a spring pour out sweet and bitter water from the same opening? Can a fig tree produce olives, my brothers, or a grapevine produce figs? Neither can a saltwater spring yield fresh water.*

When things are going well, most Christians speak words that are pleasing to God and encouraging and uplifting to others, but when things are going badly or they are offended, hurt, unhappy, and angered, they display their true colors. They speak negative, unfriendly, and destructive words toward those who have offended them. They seem to change from a "godly person" to an "ungodly person" within a short space of time. After a while, when their anger has cooled down, they go back to "normal." They pick up their "hat of Christianity" and become friendly, loving, and caring again. But they forget that their actions reflect their true identity and illustrate who they really are. When a true child of God is offended, he or she turns the matter over to God through prayer and responds with kindness, gentleness, self-control, and patience, no matter how hurt he or she may be (Galatians 5:22–23).

People who have truly experienced God's grace, mercy, transformation, power, and presence speak differently. They have a different attitude and respond to offense differently, and they always guard their heart. They use their words, or speech, to turn the situation around, and they display the heart and love of God to those around them. Why? Because they have been crucified with Christ and they no longer live, but Christ lives in them (Galatians 2:20). Carnal, ungodly, and unspiritual people use their words to incite hatred, anger, and bitterness and to bring division and destruction in the family of God. Carnal, unspiritual, and ungodly people have one thing in common: They have an attitude that produces the habit of bringing others down through discouraging words, defamation of character, slander, and libel. Their goal is to tarnish and taint other people's reputations while portraying themselves as "holy" and "righteous"—that is a spirit of witchcraft.

Let no corrupt communication proceed out of your mouth, but that which is good to the use of edifying, that it may minister grace unto the hearers. (Ephesians 4:29 KJV)

Anything spoken that does not bring life, inspiration, motivation, edification, or an increase in a person's faith and desire to live for God is not worth our attention and time. We need the word of God spoken into our lives every day because it uplifts our faith in God and brings confidence and stability in our relationship and walk with God. What you hear and listen to is what you become or act out. Determine to hear and read only the word of God, and close your ears and heart to any words that are not godly. You are what God says you are and not what others may say you are.

You are a child of God, made in God's image and called to live for Him. When you speak ungodly words, remember they are coming from the depths of your heart (who you are) and are an indication of who you really are. To change the content of your heart isn't as easy as just cleaning up your speech; it requires you to surrender your heart to the influence and control of the Holy Spirit, because out of the heart the mouth speaks. Ask constantly and every day for the power of the Holy Spirit to fill your heart so that you can develop a Christlike attitude. When the Holy Spirit purifies your heart, you will speak differently, and as a true son or daughter of God, you will speak words that bring honor and glory to God.

Controlling Your Tongue

"Those who guard their mouths and their tongues keep themselves from calamity" (Proverbs 21:23 NIV). Controlling the tongue should be as important as guarding our heart. This is because while the tongue exposes what is in our heart, it also can shape our heart. If we can change what we speak or say, we can be overcomers in Christ and win every spiritual battle. Victory in any situation lies in the power of the tongue.

When I was going through injustice, opposition, and prejudice, the Lord revealed to me that I needed to use the power of my tongue, not to curse or defend myself, but rather to declare and establish God's will and purpose for my life. As I began declaring God's will and purpose to be established in my life, I started to see God shifting my mind, heart, and focus from those who wanted to destroy me to His kingdom. And my desire to do God's will motivated me to persevere and endure hatred for the sake of proclaiming the gospel of the Lord Jesus Christ to lost souls.

The more I surrendered my tongue to the work of God, the more life came into me, and I spoke and preached from the depths of God's own heart and not from my hurts or disappointments. Furthermore, God began opening doors for me in every area of my life.

Our tongue possesses power that Satan cannot withstand, but in most cases our tongue defeats us because we use it against ourselves by telling ourselves things like these: I am a failure; I am not good enough; my marriage won't work out; my children will never be anything in life;

I am dying; I am sick, or I am going to get sick; I am poor; I don't have money; I am useless; I am unintelligent; I will never make it in life. Remember, it is not over until God says it is over; you are to speak and call things that are not as though they are (Romans 4:17). You have the power to change your life simply by declaring the word of God over your life, your marriage, family, ministry, and children.

Your Tongue Can Determine the Direction of Your Life

Proverbs 18:21 tells us, "Life and death are in the power of the tongue, and those who love it will eat its fruit." And Peter also tells us, "If you want to enjoy life and see many happy days, keep your tongue from speaking evil and your lips from telling lies" (1 Peter 3:10 NLT). As a young boy, I learned in Sunday school about life and death being in the power of the tongue. This changed what I spoke over my life and how I saw myself. Just to give you a brief picture of my life, there were (still are) ten in our family. Sometimes we went days without food, and I would walk miles to get to school and back home. But I kept declaring that my life and my family's lives would not continue this way and that my children would never go through what I went through as a kid. Today what I declared is history. God has changed my family and provided for us immensely, and I believe it is because of the power of the tongue.

When you speak the word of God over your life and your future, a shift takes place in the spiritual realm. God repositions you for success and anoints you to walk in His power to bring freedom to those who are still in captivity. When you change what you speak over your life, you will also change the direction and destiny of your life. In Ezekiel 37:4–9 God told Ezekiel to "prophesy over," or speak to, the dry bones and tell them to listen to the word of the Lord. The prophet's message was, "I will make breath enter you, and you will come to life. I will attach tendons to you and make flesh come upon you and cover you with skin; I will put breath in you, and you will come to life" (NIV). When Ezekiel prophesied, as God commanded him, there was a shifting that started to take place. There was a noise, a rattling sound, and the bones came together, bone to bone, and the bodies came to life.

Ezekiel had to speak the words to turn around the situation of the bones—from death to life. As we can see in the account, Ezekiel did not do anything special other than speak the word of God. To change any situation you might be in right now, you need to speak "life" to that situation and not death. The secret to living an overcoming and victorious life lies in your ability to control and use your tongue properly. Yes, we all have said things over our lives and over other people that we shouldn't have said. We have made many mistakes in our words and caused many people to stumble. But if we can learn to control our tongue, we can overpower the enemy in many areas of life. Our tongue is a decider of our future and destiny in life. Jesus said in Matthew 12:37, "For by your words you will be acquitted, and by your words you will be condemned" (NIV). Let your words be words that acquit you from a life situation or problem and not condemn you to failure.

A Person Who Controls His or Her Tongue Speaks with Godly Wisdom

One thing that helps us speak words of life instead of death is having godly wisdom. Wisdom plays a big role in how we speak, how we relate to people (Christians and non-Christians), and how we conduct ourselves in any given situation. God-loving, God-fearing people who are filled and influenced by the Holy Spirit are always careful and conscious of their words. They don't speak foolishly or carelessly. They are quick listeners and slow speakers (James 1:19). Their goal is to display God's glory, honor, and love. Controlling the tongue proves one's faith and relationship with God is authentic. James says, "If anyone thinks he is religious without controlling his tongue, then his religion is useless and he deceives himself" (James 1:26).

The wise King Solomon said in Proverbs 15:1, "A gentle answer deflects anger, but harsh words make tempers flare" (NLT). A rising voice and harsh words usually trigger an angry and rebellious response, but a gentle voice and wise words turn away anger and promote unity and peace. Poisonous, harsh, and unhealthy language does not solve or calm a problem and does not edify the body of believers. In fact, it only increases division and hatred and shows how foolish and lacking in godly wisdom we are.

In 2 Chronicles 1:9–11 we find the powerful account of King Solomon's request from God. God had told Solomon to ask for anything from Him and promised the king's request would be granted. King Solomon did not ask for riches, wealth, long life, honor, or the death of those who hated him, as many people would automatically do. Rather, he asked for wisdom. Why? Because it is not easy to lead people. It requires godly wisdom, not book knowledge or worldly leadership. Solomon asked God for wisdom so that he could lead and govern God's people wisely and righteously. The Bible records that God gave King Solomon wisdom and a discerning heart and also included the riches he was not even looking for because of his humble heart before God. As a result of God's gift, there was no one as wise as Solomon.

The point is that wisdom is extremely important in the Christian life. In fact, we cannot live righteously in this unrighteous world without it. Solomon understood the importance of having godly wisdom as a leader. Indeed, if a leader is not careful, he can unleash the power of his tongue (anger) upon those he leads by speaking evil and ungodly words over them, thus handing them over to the influence and attacks of Satan.

Seek godly wisdom because godly wisdom is a tree of life to those who embrace her, and happy are those who hold her tightly (Proverbs 3:18). When you have godly wisdom, your speech will be prudent, and you will use your tongue to speak life and not death.

When you are offended, hurt, or angered by people, or tempted to use your tongue unwisely, pray out the following scriptures: "I will guard my ways so that I may not sin with my tongue; I will guard my mouth with a muzzle as long as the wicked are in my presence" (Psalm 39:1); and "Let my tongue sing about your word, for all your commands are right" (Psalm 119:172 NLT). Also, remember that you are called to demonstrate the rule and reign of God's kingdom here on earth, and the best way to do that is to speak words of the kingdom, to live it out, and to encourage others to do so. Constantly speak the word of God, and don't let your heart speak out your frustrations, disappointments, or anger. Your tongue, heart, mind, and soul belong to Jesus, who has redeemed them from the power and influence of Satan, so they must function to bring glory and honor to the kingdom of God and to His holy name. If we want to see reformation, transformation, and revival in the nations, we need to speak only the life-reviving and transforming word of God.

Your Tongue Must Always Speak the Word of God

Controlling your tongue doesn't mean you say nothing. It means you speak what is important, life-changing, uplifting, uniting, and honoring to God. When you use your tongue to speak the word of God, it changes lives, brings transformation, gives hope to the hopeless, and releases people from their chains of bondage. The word of God is powerful, because it is simply God in action. John 1:1 says, "In the beginning was the Word, and the Word was with God, and the Word was God." To speak the word of God is to speak God Himself, and when you speak God in or to any circumstance, the kingdom of darkness crumbles and life blossoms.

Hebrews 4:12 tells us about the power of the spoken word of God: "For the word of God is living and effective and sharper than any double-edged sword, penetrating as far as the separation of soul and spirit, joints and marrow. It is able to judge the ideas and thoughts of the heart." When we speak the word of God, it brings life, crushes demonic forces, penetrates strongholds, dismantles curses and every high place in our lives, and establishes the presence of God in us. And where the presence of God is, darkness can never exist. We must always speak the word of God because we are born again, not of corruptible seed, but of incorruptible seed, by the word of God, which is living and abides forever (1 Peter 1:23).

Every powerful thing God does, or ever did, is accomplished by the power of His word. His word has the power to create something new or revive something that is dead. Ezekiel spoke the word of God to bring to life the dry and dead bones (Ezekiel 37:4). Jonah preached the word of God and called the people of Nineveh to repentance. When the people believed God's message, they repented, and God withdrew His burning anger and wrath (Jonah 3:5–10). Jesus healed, raised the dead, and restored the sight of the blind by the power of the word of God. The list goes on and on. It is only through the power of the spoken word of God that we can change the world, change circumstances, and win spiritual battles. The word of God is deeply connected to the power of God. We cannot have God's power without speaking the word of God. Through the word of God we have the power to forgive the sins of people. As Jesus said, "If you forgive the sins of any, they are forgiven them; if you retain the sins of any, they are retained" (John 20:23).

As disciples of our Lord Jesus Christ, God has bestowed upon us the authority and power to forgive people. If we don't forgive them, they will not be forgiven. This shows us how much power God has given us through forgiveness. Just through our words, we have the power to set people free from the kingdom of darkness to enter the kingdom of God. Satan knows that when we say, "I forgive you" from the depths of our heart, people are indeed forgiven. That is why He doesn't want us to forgive. He likes keeping people in bondage. Let us not help him achieve this. Let us forgive, forgive, and keep forgiving. When we speak words such as "I forgive you" or "I bless you" to people, we are releasing them and ourselves from the influence of the Devil and commanding a blessing upon our own lives. With the power of our tongue, we can stir people to freedom, life, and peace or to bondage. Our desire should be to use our tongue to bless and proclaim liberty and release to the captives from the hands of the Evil One.

Jesus' words in Matthew 16:19 also show us that God has given us the authority to bind or loose: "I will give you the keys of the kingdom of heaven, and whatever you bind on earth is already bound in heaven, and whatever you loose on earth is already loosed in heaven." It is no wonder Proverbs 18:21 tells us, "Life and death are in the power of the tongue, and those who love it will eat its fruit." Your tongue is powerful. Satan will do everything possible to stop you from saying the words, "I forgive you," because whatever you forgive has also been forgiven by God. Forgiveness is a dynamic power and a weapon of spiritual warfare. When you forgive those who have wronged you, the enemy is defeated.

While on the cross, Jesus used the weapon of forgiveness to defeat the enemy. He forgave both those who crucified Him (Luke 23:34) and the penitent thief (Luke 23:39–43), and through His death, He paid for our sins and forgave all our iniquities. So why shouldn't we also forgive the iniquities of others? Why keep people in bondage by not forgiving them when God wants them free? He has not only taken away our sins but also wiped them out completely, without keeping a record of any of them. If we forgive those who sin against us, the greater benefit is that our heavenly Father will also forgive us. "For I will forgive their wickedness and will remember their sins no more" (Hebrews 8:12 NIV).

If He wanted, God could remember our sins, but He has chosen not to. The same way God has chosen to forgive our sins and not remember them, we too have the power within us to forgive and not remember the trespasses of people. Sadly, however, we often choose to remember every detail of every wrong done to us.

You have the power to forgive. Use it to forgive others, and you will experience freedom, joy, and a renewed fellowship with God and with people. It is my prayer that as you read this book, God will help you to understand that forgiveness is a powerful weapon of spiritual warfare; with it you can defeat Satan (the father of evil), get your life back on track, and enjoy a peaceful and fulfilled life in the presence of the almighty God.

Your hour has arrived to move away from your past and enter into the destiny God designed just for you before you were even born. No mountain is too big, wide, high, or strong for the Lord. Every mountain bows at the mention of His powerful name and by the power of His word. Any mountain of unforgiveness, bitterness, resentment, hatred, anger, and rejection in your life must bow down to the authority and power of the name of Jesus. It is your time to shine with the radiant presence of God, so rejoice and be glad because the Lord is doing a new thing in your life! By speaking the word of God over your life, you can reverse every curse that has been spoken over your life, future, marriage, family, children, husband, or wife. When you have forgiven your enemies, discovered the mystery power of forgiveness, and learned to control your tongue, you will begin to walk in the impossible, the supernatural, and the anointing of God, and you will defeat all the tactics of the Devil against your life.

In the next chapter we will look at offense and how Satan uses it to get us off track, living in defeat, and no longer walking in the promises of God. Offense is the Devil's weapon to stop us from moving forward.

Chapter 4

OFFENSE: A BAIT OF THE DEVIL

"Woe to the world because of offenses. For offenses must come, but woe to that man by whom the offense comes." (Matthew 18:7)

"Offenses will certainly come, but woe to the one they come through! It would be better for him if a millstone were hung around his neck and he were thrown into the sea than for him to cause one of these little ones to stumble. Be on your guard. If your brother sins, rebuke him, and if he repents, forgive him. And if he sins against you seven times in a day, and comes back to you seven times, saying, 'I repent,' you must forgive him." (Luke 17:1–4)

IN THIS CHAPTER WE ARE GOING TO UNMASK THE EVIL WEAPON OF OFFENSE SO THAT we can learn to defeat Satan's tactics and recover what he has stolen from us. Offense is one of the root causes of anger, hatred, resentment, rebellion, and division in the community of believers, which eventually lead to the spirit or atmosphere of unforgiveness. Furthermore, offense is what causes many people to stumble in their walk with God and even walk away from His presence. In this chapter we are going to discover how to deal with offense, Satan's weapon for destroying dreams, gifts, talents, marriages, friendships, relationships, and churches. Although the almighty and powerful Jesus Christ has already defeated him, Satan still uses simple weapons such as offense, sin, unforgiveness, hatred, and bitterness to trap people and make them fall away from the presence and power of God into his presence and the influence of darkness and death.

There is a clear reason why Satan wants you offended. He knows that when you are offended and you respond to offense by being disgruntled, bitter, and angry and you let that anger control you, he can lead you to do the unthinkable so that the power of God in you is disarmed and your spiritual life and growth are paralyzed. Many people today are unhappy, unforgiving, and bitter because of offense, and as a consequence they are not walking in the power of God and in the power of His anointing. Furthermore, they don't have the power to pray effective prayers, to love other people, and to function in their calling and gifts.

To recover what the enemy has stolen and keeps stealing from you, you need to discover the gimmicks he utilizes to rob you of the word of God, your courage, your faith, your happiness, and your destiny. Knowing the full extent of the power of offense and its evil, Jesus warned His disciples in Matthew 18:7, "Woe to the world because of offenses. For offenses must come, but woe to that man by whom the offense comes." Jesus warned that offense will come, and because of it many people will stumble. Our first objective is to find out what offense is. Only then will we grasp how evil it is and avoid willingly offending others or allowing offense to come into the world through us.

Offense Defined

What is offense? Why does it seem to be a bigger problem in this generation than in previous ones? And why has it destroyed so many moves of God in churches, as well as in families, marriages, and relationships? To help us define what offense really is, let us turn to the Greek word for offense: *skandalon*. *Skandalon* (the verb form is *skandalizo*) means snare or stumbling block. Originally, it referred to the trigger of a trap, which held the bait. Offense is simply an act, or series of acts, that leads or traps another person into sin or triggers the desire to sin. It is like a rock placed along the pathway for the purpose of tripping one passing by. When people speak offensive or abusive words to a person, the Devil seeks to use those words to trigger anger and bitterness and develop a grudge in the heart of the offended person so that the Devil can neutralize the power of God in that person's life and eventually lead him or her away from God's presence, guidance, and kingdom.

Thus, it is important for Christians to understand that offense is a trap of the Devil that is designed to make people stumble in their faith and their walk with God. To offend someone is simply to put a stumbling block in that person's life to entice the person to sin. For this reason Jesus warned us in Luke 17:1–2, "Offenses will certainly come, but woe to the one they come through! It would be better for him if a millstone were hung around his neck and he were thrown into the sea than for him to cause one of these little ones to stumble." Countless people have given up on God because they were offended. But as a Christian you need to understand that "offense has come" and the Devil will do everything within his limited power to offend you so that he can take you away from God and destroy your testimony and trust in Him. According to Jesus, a person who offends the children of God and causes them to stumble would be better off being weighted down and thrown into the sea because he or she is worthless to the advancement of the kingdom of God and to winning souls for God.

When the Bible speaks of a "stumbling block," it refers to behaviors or attitudes that lead another person to fall into sin. We must always be careful not to cause other people to stumble in their walk with God because of our ungodly behavior or attitude. Our attitude toward others must always reflect the heart, spirit, character, and nature of God. In fact, we must always display a Christlike attitude because Christ lives in us and we live in Him. Our desire and passion should be to act as a bridge for people to cross over from the kingdom of darkness into the kingdom of light and not to be a stumbling block through senseless, unworthy, and ungodly words and acts. Offense is such a simple weapon, yet it is very powerful and successful in pulling people away from God and from the family of believers.

Offense is cruel and evil. Because of it, many people have committed spiritual or physical suicide. It paralyzes people's passion, desire, and hunger for intimacy with God. We are called not to offend other believers in Christ but to motivate, inspire, empower, and encourage them to live for God in a world already offended by the gospel of our Lord Jesus Christ. Divine judgment awaits those who offend Christ's followers or cause them to stumble in their faith. God is very serious about removing anything that makes His people stumble in their faith, because as we have already stated, offense is a snare and a weapon Satan uses to pull people away from God and destroy God's work in the hearts of believers.

When you are offended, do not rush to react or respond, because when you respond in anger or in a negative way, you may fall into the trap of the Devil, which is sin. Guarding your heart against offense and any other ungodly things in your life is necessary for you to continue to walk in the presence and anointing of God. If you want to attract more of God's power, anointing, and presence in your life, you must avoid offending others, and you must walk in forgiveness at all times. When you are offended or wronged, forgive without limits, so that you do not fall into the enemy's trap of unforgiveness. First Peter 5:8 says, "Be alert and of sober mind. Your enemy the devil prowls around like a roaring lion looking for someone to devour" (NIV).

Offense Is an Obstacle to the Rule and Reign of God in the Hearts of People

As Jesus was giving the interpretation of the parable of the wheat and the weeds, He stated, "The Son of man shall send forth his angels, and they shall gather out of his kingdom all things that offend, and them which do iniquity" (Matthew 13:41 KJV). "Things that offend" are obstacles to God's rule and reign in the lives of people. That is why God hates offense and He will judge anybody who offends others purposely. It is one thing to rebuke or point out sin in people's lives with the intention of restoring them to fellowship with God and His people. It is another thing to point out sin in people's lives with an attitude of self-righteousness or with the motive of hurting them. That is not a godly way of reaching out to the lost or to sinful brothers and sisters. We must reach out to them with Christlike passion to pull them toward God and not away from Him. This does not mean we become "seeker sensitive" and preach a diluted and non-convicting message, but it does mean we are to preach with a heart of compassion and empathy for lost souls and take them one step at a time toward God. We can't rush to give solid food to infants but must develop their intestines step by step with soft food so that one day they will be strong and stable enough to eat solid food. Jesus did not rush His disciples to do greater things. He first took them into discipleship training so that He could develop them into spiritual giants and powerful men of God.

In Matthew 18:7–14 Jesus told His disciples of two ways to cause others to sin or stumble: through offense (temptation) or through demeaning them. Other causes of stumbling include false teaching, or the traditions of man, and promotion of ungodly living (Revelation 2:14). As ambassadors of Jesus Christ, we must do our best through the power of the Holy Spirit to get rid of every stumbling block and to stop anyone who could cause others to stumble in their faith or lead them into sin. The crazy and out-of-context teaching of so-called "extreme grace" has led many into the bondage of sin. We are to deal with sin in us so that the true grace of God can uproot it and empower us to faithfully and powerfully live for God. True grace empowers people to live in the purity of God's righteousness. It does not make them comfortable remaining in sin. Jesus has defeated the obstacle of sin and death, and now we are free to live for Him and do His works without condemnation. Offense is what hinders people from allowing God to effectively rule and reign in their lives.

The only way we should offend this sinful world and its people is by preaching the gospel of Jesus Christ and calling people to repent and turn away from their wickedness. We should never be apologetic about rebuking sin and proclaiming the message of the cross. The offense God is against is the offense of making other people fall into sin because of ungodly attitudes, lifestyles, or speech. Let us not confuse the two issues. Offending people with our ungodly ways is not the same as offending them with the convicting gospel of the Lord Jesus Christ. If people are offended by the preaching of the truth or the convicting power of the gospel, that is not our problem. If they are offended because we are arrogant and unwise in our actions, that *is* our problem, and we can expect God to punish us for making them stumble.

Jesus—A Stumbling Block to the Religious Unbelievers

Isaiah 8:14–15, which is quoted several times in the New Testament, pictures Jesus Christ as the "rock of offense":

He will be a sanctuary; but for the two houses of Israel, He will be a stone to stumble over and a rock to trip over, and a trap and a snare to the inhabitants of Jerusalem. Many will stumble over these; they will fall and be broken; they will be snared and captured.

When we look deeply into the life and ministry of Jesus Christ, we find something very interesting. Jesus did not offend people, and particularly the religious leaders of His day, through an ungodly lifestyle or character. Rather, He offended them by preaching the gospel of the cross, and He was that gospel, for He is the way to God the Father. Furthermore, He was the promised Messiah who had come from God to redeem the Jewish people and all humanity from the power of sin and death. But Jesus was rejected by His people because He did not meet their criteria; He was not the "military Messiah" they were expecting to come and liberate them from the power and oppression of the Roman Empire. Because of this He became an "offense," or "stumbling block," to the houses of Israel and Judah. Yet even though people were offended at Him, beat Him up, spat at Him, called Him names, and crucified Him, His great character and forgiving heart was illustrated on the cross when He cried out to God, "Father, forgive them, because they do not know what they are doing" (Luke 23:34).

Even in the most agonizing and painful situation, Jesus chose to forgive. In the end He died to save those who were offended by Him so that they could have eternal life. To the religious people of Jesus' day, the cross, or the idea of a crucified Messiah, was an offense and foolishness, for it signaled weakness. Furthermore, the message of the cross was offensive to many because it declared that Jesus Christ was and is the only atoning Sacrifice and the only way to be forgiven and made right with God (John 14:6; Acts 4:12; 1 Corinthians 1:23). The people's rejection of Jesus Christ caused them to experience Him as a stumbling stone, but to those who accepted Him, He became the stone upon which they would build their fellowship and relationship with God and live righteous lives in Him. Christ crucified was a stumbling block (*skandalon,* offense) to the Jewish expectations. As for the Gentiles, who had no messianic expectations, a crucified Savior was foolishness and didn't make any sense at all. Because of unbelief, even the most religious people could not experience the rule and reign of God.

Unbelief—A Stumbling Block to Experiencing God's Power
In 1 Corinthians 1:21–25, the apostle Paul stated:

> *For since, in God's wisdom, the world did not know God through wisdom, God was pleased to save those who believe through the foolishness of the message preached. For the Jews ask for signs and the Greeks seek wisdom, but we preach Christ crucified, a stumbling block to the Jews and foolishness to the Gentiles. Yet to those who are called, both Jews and Greeks, Christ is God's power and God's wisdom, because God's foolishness is wiser than human wisdom, and God's weakness is stronger than human strength.*

Many people stumble on Jesus, the Rock of Ages, because of their unbelief and disobedience to the gospel message of the cross; consequently, they fail to experience God's power unto salvation. Peter wrote, "And 'A stone of stumbling, and a rock of offense.' They stumble because they disobey the word, as they were destined to do" (1 Peter 2:8 ESV). When we preach the message of the cross, or the gospel of Jesus Christ, and people are offended, we are not to apologize, give up, or give in to preaching a humanistic, materialistic, diluted, and polluted gospel that appeals to the fleshly desires of mankind. Instead, we must preach the pure gospel of Jesus Christ that brings spiritual transformation, change, reformation, and revival.

Our lives and actions must always match our belief. We must practice what we preach so that we lead people to Christ and not away from Him. Let the light of God in you offend the darkness that is in the world; do not needlessly offend the world with an inconsistent and ungodly life. I have seen with my own eyes how Christians can lead people away from God or prevent them from living for God because of their bad character and attitude. I pray that as you read this book, you will allow the Holy Spirit to help you develop the character of God so that you will inspire and make others desire to live for God because of the Spirit of God in you.

Offense Has Come into the World—Overcome It with Good

Offense has come into the world just as Jesus prophesied in Matthew 18:7, saying, "Offenses must come, but woe to that man by whom the offense comes." If there is a disease that is slowly eating up the church and many believers in Christ, it is offense. There is not a single week goes by that I do not meet a person who has left a church or churches because of offense or while still in the church has been offended because of something someone said or did to him or her. The church is not as effective and powerful as it should be in the world because the people who are the church are buried under the power of bitterness and anger—much to the delight of the Devil.

Satan loves to see people offended so that he can work through bitterness, anger, and unforgiveness to bully, manipulate, control, and influence people to commit ungodly acts and disrupt the flow and power of God in the church. Knowing how to deal with and respond to offense is crucial if we are to be channels through whom God brings change, reformation, and transformation to this world. We also must desire to learn how to avoid injuring or offending people because of our careless speech or tendencies. In the next chapter, we will see how we can deal with offense and how we also can avoid offending others or making them stumble because of unwisely chosen words. But first, let's take a look at how offense tests our level of faith and maturity in God.

Offense Will Test Your Level of Faith and Maturity in God

Offenses, or trials in life, do not come only to lure you away from your faith in God or away from His presence; they come also to test your spiritual stability and faith and trust in God. You are not yet proven solid in Christ or stable if you have not yet been tried, tested, grilled, and toasted by life situations. And you will never know or find out how truly stable you are in Christ if you have not been through the fire. True soldiers in Christ who are stable, full of endurance, persistent, caring, and loving are those who have been through the fire of offense and opposition and come out of it without burning out or giving up. When you have been tested and tried and you pass the testing, no mountains, no hills, no valleys, and no circumstances can move you or shake you or make you doubt the power of God, because you have been through it all and God has been with you in it, and there is nothing to fear.

> *There is wonderful joy ahead, even though you must endure many trials for a little while. These trials will show that your faith is genuine. It is being tested as fire tests and purifies gold—though your faith is far more precious than mere gold. So when your faith remains strong through many trials, it will bring you much praise and glory and honor on the day when Jesus Christ is revealed to the whole world.* (1 Peter 1:6–7 NLT)

Here Peter was writing to the Jewish Christians who had been driven out of Jerusalem and were experiencing persecution for their faith. He encouraged and comforted them in his letter, but what is so significant here is that he tells them, "These trials will show that your faith is genuine." Many people fail the test when they go through trials because they give up so quickly, and thus give up on God, when things are going badly. This is because their faith has never been through the fire of persecution, pressure, offense, or opposition. In order for your faith to be genuine and strong, you need to go through trials. True faith in God does not budge. It does not know how to surrender and does not question God's power and ability to save in times of severe storms. It stands strong in times of trouble and proves itself by trusting the God of all power to demonstrate His extraordinary power in any situation. True faith allows God to be who He says He is and does not doubt that He is quite capable of transforming a bad experience into a good one.

Various trials in your life, including offense, can develop the genuineness of your faith and bring praise, glory, and honor to the name of God—but only if you respond with a godly attitude and not a worldly attitude. Trials come to test your faith and trust in God, and when your faith remains strong through many trials, you will be victorious and declared a true son or daughter of God. You have no proven faith until your faith is tried and tested. Many Christians start with great zeal and passion for Jesus Christ and for His Word, but when trials knock on their doors, they falter and disappear from the presence of God. You need to be tested in order to move to the next chapter or season of your life in God. Struggles, trials, offense, and persecution refine and strengthen your faith, consequently making you a useful and stable vessel of God. As you pass every test of offense or opposition, you grow from strength to strength and from glory to glory. It is when you are under stressful situations that your outward mask is removed and what lurks inside is revealed. Opposition or offense will test you and reveal your personality and character so that people will see who you really are and what you are made of.

When you are going through trials, don't panic or say to God, "Why me, Lord?" as many people do. Instead, respond to trials with confidence, reverence, courage, perseverance, and endurance, expecting God to get you through it without any scars on your life. What doesn't kill you makes you stronger and perfects your faith in God, but above all, it gives you a powerful testimony that can bring deliverance to many people in your life. When you have gone through the tempest, you can sail through any storms without being shipwrecked. Don't run away from the storms of life, but go through them with unshakable faith and trust in the power and ability of God so that you can be prepared and equipped to face any task ahead of you. Here is the attitude you should have when you are going through trials or great suffering: (1) Expect trials (1 Peter 4:12), (2) be thankful to God for the great privilege of suffering for Christ (1 Peter 4:13–18), and (3) trust the Lord for deliverance (1 Peter 4:19).

Always remember that as long as you are here on earth, you will experience some difficult times. However, when you suffer for doing what is right before God, God will honor you. He will let His glory shine over you, give you strength, and deliver you. If you are currently going through a difficult time in your life, understand that no storm or season lasts forever, but is just for a limited period. Also, remember that following Christ is a costly commitment and business. It is not for the fainthearted, short-tempered, or easily offended but only for those who have the character of Jesus Christ. Trials can refine your faith and stability in God, but how you respond to them will determine whether they destroy you or make you stronger in Christ.

Tested, Tried, and Proven—to Be Stable in Christ

Until your faith is tested, you are not ready to live like a soldier of Christ. Almost every person you will meet in life will bring some kind of challenge to your faith and stability in God. That is why it is important to walk in forgiveness—so that you do not falter when you are tested. Whatever you may be going through today, God is going to use it to train you for spiritual battles. Through the trials of offense, He will prepare your life for greater things to come in service for His kingdom, so stand strong and don't give up. Furthermore, offense will not only test your level of faith in God but also your level of love for and patience with the lost. Those who pass the test and persevere in faith while suffering persecution or trials are filled with compassion and love for people, and they can help many others who are going through difficult moments in life. When you have been through the fire of offense, you become a stable vessel God can use to help others and to motivate them to stand the tests and so prove their faith and loyalty to the cross.

It is not pleasant to go through trials, but as we have already stated, they can refine and redefine your Christianity and your trust in God. Nobody wants to buy a product that has no quality, or one that has not been tried, tested, or proven. That is why listening to people preach about something they have never experienced in life seldom brings freedom or makes an impact. We build our lives on Jesus Christ (Isaiah 28:16) and on the foundation of the apostles because they have been tested and proven unshakable and immovable by the temptations and storms of life. A person who desires to live a powerful and impactful life does not model his or her life on an unstable or inconsistent person but on those who have been through the fire and have come out strong and proven their stability in their life and faith in Christ.

Offense and Unforgiveness Can Hinder Your Breakthrough in Life

While offense tests our spiritual stability, love, faith, and trust in God, it also can hinder our breakthrough in life. This is because when we are offended we can become so focused on the hurt done to us that we ignore what God wants to do through us with forgiveness. Offense that is not dealt with or is taken personally can hinder us from experiencing a breakthrough in life and from working together in unity with other believers in Christ to advance the kingdom of God. Thus, responding properly to offense will allow us to thrive and flourish in our Christian lives and be great ambassadors of Christ to those around us.

> *"If you are offering your gift on the altar, and there you remember that your brother has something against you, leave your gift there in front of the altar. First go and be reconciled with your brother, and then come and offer your gift."* (Matthew 5:23–24)

These are profound verses. Most people like to think that the only thing that matters in our Christian lives is our personal "relationship with God," and they give little importance to our relationship with other believers or people in general. Thus, we tend to say or do things to other people that demean and devalue them. Absolutely, God is the most important Person in our lives, but that same God demands that we respect each and every person because all people are created in His image. The apostle John wrote in 1 John 4:20, "Whoever claims to love God yet hates a brother or sister is a liar. For whoever does not love their brother and sister, whom they have seen, cannot love God, whom they have not seen" (NIV). God has placed such a high value on every human being that He sacrificed His own Son to save them (John 3:16). Such is the magnitude of God's love for us.

Our relationship with other people is a reflection of our true love and relationship and fellowship with God. Because our relationship with other people mirrors our relationship with God, Jesus instructed His followers to seek reconciliation with anyone who might have a grudge against them before they made an offering to God (Matthew 5:23–24). This meant that even if a person was already in the middle of presenting a sacrifice to God at the temple, that person was to halt the ceremony and seek forgiveness and/or reconciliation first. This shows us that God is deeply interested in His people worshiping Him with a pure heart, a contrite spirit, and a genuine love for both God and His created people. What we should understand here is why this interruption was so very significant. Most of Jesus' original audience lived away from Jerusalem, which means they would have to abandon their gift at the temple altar and travel, perhaps for days, to reach their community in Galilee or elsewhere to seek reconciliation before making another lengthy journey back to Jerusalem to complete their sacrifice.

Your breakthrough in life takes place when you clear things out of your path that might hinder or stop it from becoming a reality. Unforgiveness in response to offense definitely can hinder God from acting on your behalf or from accepting your sacrifices or requests. Above all, broken relationships can hinder your relationship and fellowship with God. If you have a grievance or a problem with a friend or your Christian brother or sister, you should immediately resolve that problem so that nothing is standing in your way when you worship God or pray for a particular issue that needs God's intervention. The great lesson we learn in Matthew 5:23–24 is that God takes seriously our relationship with other people because the way we relate to people demonstrates that God indeed lives in us and we in Him.

As Christians, we must always remember that each of us is a picture of God's character. That is why people question the reality of God in us when we act in a bad way. Before presenting your offering to God or prayer request to Him, search your heart and make sure you have settled all your grievances with people and made peace with them so that you can offer an acceptable and pure sacrifice before God. Otherwise, the repercussion may be that your sacrifice or request is not accepted by God.

Most unanswered prayers are due to the attitude and spirit in which we petition God. For example, when we dutifully ask God to send revival in the church and yet we are full of hatred toward each other, we may as well forget it. God will not waste His precious anointing on vessels that do not have a contrite heart. We must be willing to humble ourselves, forget our ego, and reconcile with each other so that we can walk in the fullness of God's presence. Christianity is lived in a community of believers and not in isolation. Our relationship with other people matters a great deal to God because He cares about people and not just about us.

God Cares about Other People Too

You might say, "Who cares if I offend people?" Well, God cares very much because your careless words can lead other people, especially new or weaker Christians, astray. Ephesians 6:4 also warns us not to "provoke," or "stir up anger," in our children (children of faith) but to bring them up in the nurture and admonition of the Lord. Colossians 3:21 also says, "Fathers, do not exasperate your children, so they won't become discouraged." Offense discourages, demoralizes, and dismantles people's faith and trust, not only in God but also in other people. Deliberate provocation stirs up anger and disunity in the body of Christ. As children of the light, we must have a godly concern for other people and live to inspire them to do the will of God and to live for Him. Nevertheless, if people are offended because we are preaching the true Word of God or sharing the gospel of our Lord Jesus Christ in love, that is not a big deal.

Share the Word of God with people, not in arrogance or self-righteousness, but in the Spirit of God's love and compassion for the lost. Jesus Christ is compassionate toward the lost. We too are to be compassionate and preach the good news of the kingdom to the lost in the light of God's love and mercy. Sin has already condemned sinful people to death. We are called and anointed to set them free and not to condemn them. As we have already stated, we are not to be super "seeker-sensitive" people who avoid preaching the convicting and truthful Word of God; rather, we are to use our God-given wisdom to win the lost to God. Offense is Satan's weapon to lead people away from entering into the kingdom of God, and we must never use it to try to make people feel guilty for their sin. God does not use the same strategy as the enemy; He uses mercy, grace, and love to win lost souls to Him.

At the top of the list of things that hinder us from walking in our inheritance from God and advancing His kingdom here on earth is the

Devil's weapon of offense. Thus, it is important for us to understand that careless and offensive words we speak to people have the power to cause them to fall or stumble in their faith in God because they entice people to sin in their anger. The Bible strongly warns us that we will give an account for every careless word we speak. By our words we will be justified or condemned (Matthew 12:36–37). James 1:19–20 advises us to be quick to hear, slow to speak, and slow to anger because words spoken in anger, exasperation, or under pressure, or even out of excitement can offend people and cause them to stumble in their faith.

At the same time, we must remember that rebuking brothers or sisters in the Lord and in love is not the same as offending them. To rebuke is to express disapproval of a sinful behavior in a person, while to offend is to hurt or wound a person in such a way that he or she is tempted to sin in anger. Yes, some believers in Christ may be offended when you disapprove of their sinful actions by pointing them to the Word of God in love, but your conscience will be clear, for you will help some to turn away from their ungodly ways and to turn to God. Having godly wisdom is very important when you are dealing with people because it can help you speak out of love for a person and not out of hatred.

The Purpose of Rebuke

People who are offended by our rebuke often are not offended because we have wrongly accused them but because of our self-righteous attitude. We should always check our attitude and our spirit before we rebuke a person, because our attitude can lead a person either to God or away from Him. There is an old saying that goes like this: "It is not what you say but how you say it that matters." But again, some people will be offended regardless of what you say and how you say it because we are living in an easily offended generation. Satan has unleashed the power of offense upon the earth today. People nowadays are easily angered, upset, and made resentful over little things because Satan is working to keep as many people as possible away from the presence of God through offense.

It is important to remember that "offenses" are unavoidable in life. In fact, each and every day Satan targets his arrows of offense at the upright in heart in order to bring them down and destroy the work of God in them. Most people react to offenses with strong resentment because they are not operating in the Spirit but in their flesh. Living in the Spirit of God and in His Word at all times will help you avoid responding to offense in a negative way. When you live your life under the leading of the Holy Spirit of God, you become dead to Satan's arrows of evil. Furthermore, when you live your life under the power of the Holy Spirit, you will easily walk in love instead of in hatred, in joy instead of in sadness, in peace instead of in discord, in patience instead of in agitation, in kindness instead of in hostility, and in faithfulness instead of in faithlessness (Galatians 5:22).

The purpose of rebuking sinners should be to get them to repent of their sinful ways and to restore them back to God, not to show them how sinful or devilish they are. We are to point people to Jesus so that He alone can set them free. Judgmental attitudes do not help in bringing healing and restoration. When we preach the Word of God in love to those living in sin, we demonstrate that we are in the light and there is no cause for stumbling (1 John 2:10). We cannot emphasize enough that relationships with fellow believers or people in general are key indicators of whether we are walking in the light (in God) or in the darkness (in Satan). If we love God, we will also love people.

It is true that some people are not so easy to love because of their attitude or way of doing things, but we must clearly understand that we are not to love people because they have a great attitude or because of what they have done for us; rather, we are to love people because they were created in God's image and because the God of love lives and dwells in us. We don't love the sin or the bad behavior of people, but we love *them* because God loves them. If we can grasp this, we will forgive people easily, be free from bitterness and anger, and love as God loves— with no strings attached. Sadly, offense always stands in our way and makes it difficult to love and forgive people.

Things to Remember

We must learn how to deal with offense if we are to demonstrate the character of God. In the next chapter, we are going to focus on how we can effectively deal with the "bait of offense." For now, however, let us review some important principles related to offense.

When you are offended, or persecuted, or opposed, always remember that Satan is looking to lure you into sin. Do not let your anger consume you because this will position you to be influenced by Satan. The other important thing you should know about offense is that it can prevent you from purely worshiping, praising, and glorifying God in Spirit and in truth. You cannot offer a pure and acceptable sacrifice before God from a heart filled with bitterness or anger.

If you want to see the glorious power of God in your life, you must allow the Holy Spirit to empty your heart of all bitterness, unforgiveness, anger, and hatred. The reason we are not walking in the authentic power of God is because as a people we have been consumed by anger and hatred. We might pretend to love each other, but deep down in our hearts we do not love one another at all. We need to go back to the basics and flush out everything in our system that is not of God so that we can be the people God is looking for in these end times to bring His glory, power, and love to lost souls.

Finally, if you don't deal with offense God's way, it will be impossible for you to effectively walk in your God-given vision and dreams because offense is a "bait of Satan" to lure you from God's vision and destiny for your life. Offense is like a parasite that occupies and infiltrates a person's mind and heart, causing one to act or speak in an ungodly way. A bitter response to situations underscores the need for the influence of the Holy Spirit in our lives.

Knowing how to deal with or respond to offense will help you to walk in forgiveness. You have been forgiven by God so that you can forgive others. In fact, forgiving others is deeply connected to God's forgiveness of our sins and to our relationship with Him (Matthew 6:14–15). When we flush away things that keep us from God and from walking in His power, no trap or stumbling block can stop us from doing the mighty works of God here on earth. This is why, when Peter took Jesus aside and rebuked Him, saying, in effect, "God forbid that you will be arrested or killed" (Matthew 16:22), Jesus responded to Peter by saying, "Get away from me, Satan! You are a dangerous trap to me.

You are seeing things merely from a human point of view, not from God's" (Matthew 16:23 NLT). Peter was not "Satan," but his statement and attitude at that moment was influenced by Satan to trap Jesus by tempting Him to evade the cross. Jesus, however, flushed him out and fulfilled His mission on the cross.

How many people have been tricked and trapped into not living passionately for God by the Devil, who through the voices of man brings discouragement, distortion, insult, and opposition? And many also have been pulled away from God because of the spirit of unforgiveness. Let me tell you this: God wants you to use the power of your tongue to tell every problem in your life that stops you from living for Him and from passionately serving Him to get behind you—now. Furthermore, in the power and in the anointed name of Jesus Christ, He wants you to tell offense and the spirit of unforgiveness in your life to get behind you. Through offense Satan desperately wants to steal God's glory and honor, and he does so by using people to offend each other.

You need to say, "Offense, you are a dangerous trap to me, to my life in God, to my calling in Christ, and to my future, and I therefore command you to leave in Jesus' name." As you declare that, take a practical step to walk in forgiveness and to live through the power of the Holy Spirit. The Holy Spirit will help you to respond to offense. Again, you cannot stop people from speaking evil words against you or otherwise offending you, but you have the power to stop yourself from retaliating in an evil way.

So let's go now to chapter 5 and learn how we can effectively deal with offense.

Chapter 5

EFFECTIVE WAYS TO DEAL WITH OFFENSE

ONE OF THE MOST IMPORTANT THINGS TO KNOW AND REMEMBER AS A CHRISTIAN LIVING here on earth is that offense will come. As Jesus predicted, you will be offended by people of this world. Unfortunately, you also will be offended by some religious people of this world. Don't be surprised, moved, or shaken when those who are close to you or those who appear very spiritual offend you. Always keep in mind, however, that your response is critical to the demonstration of the nature of God and of His kingdom. You may be the first picture or image of God people see, so how you respond to a difficult situation and present yourself can either lift up the image and glory of God or bring it down. When you are offended, you need to know that God's image and glory is at stake and not just your pride or ego. Most people are more protective of their pride and ego than they are of the image and glory of God. But remember, the way you respond to offense can bring either glory and honor to God and thereby win people over to Him, or bring shame and damage to His name.

Some people reject God because of the bad experiences they have suffered at the hands of a few "Christians," or those who claim to be children of God. Satan deliberately causes people to say things or do things against you that will trouble your heart and bring offense to you so that he can influence you to respond in a manner that brings dishonor and damage to the name of God and His kingdom, and so turn people away from His presence. Having a true fear of God and a desire in your heart to see His name glorified and many people come into His kingdom should restrain you from responding to offense in an ungodly way or out of anger. By *fear* I mean reverential awe and obedient respect for the covenant-keeping God.

When you have a reverential awe of God and love for people, you will do everything possible through the power of the Holy Spirit in you to forgive people and deal with offense in a way that brings glory to the name of God—even if it costs you your ego, pride, and dignity. True children of God find their dignity and pride in God and not in themselves. Consequently, they don't care what people do to their flesh. They have their being in Christ and would rather defend the name of God in humility than defend themselves by avenging the wrongs done to them. When you have this mind-set and attitude in your heart, you can deal with offense effectively because it is no longer about you but about the reputation of the Lord Yahweh. If you truly love God and are born of Him, you will lay down your pride and ego and respond to offense with forgiveness. In so doing, you will maintain the honor and dignity of the name of God.

Satan is after two things: Destroying God's reputation and honor and destroying your faith in God and His powerful name. Understand this: Forgiveness is not really about you or the person you are forgiving; it is about restoring and maintaining the reputation, honor, glory, and dignity of God. Yes, forgiving another person takes that person out of the shackles or prison of a curse and also opens doors for you, but at the center of forgiveness are God's reputation, honor, and glory.

When God sent His Son, Jesus Christ, to die, three important things happened: (1) He paid the price for our sins through His blood so that our sins could be forgiven; (2) we were redeemed from the power of sin and death; and (3) God's honor, dignity, and reputation were restored. Through the forgiveness of our sins, our relationship and fellowship with God were restored and our power and authority through the name of Jesus Christ—the name above every other name—was reestablished. Thus, we have power and authority over the kingdom of darkness through the name of Jesus. The name of Jesus (Jesus Himself) is so very important to our calling and life as Christians. It is His name that we represent and carry everywhere we go, so if we are not careful, we can tarnish His name and bring shame to it through our flawed character, wrong attitude, or unforgiving heart.

The honor and reputation of God's name should be far more important and more desirable to us than our own dignity. The next time you are offended, think before you respond, because you are an image of God. When people see you, they should see God in you; when they listen to you, they should hear the voice of God; and when they are with you, they should sense the Spirit of God and not the spirit of the world. As you learn in this chapter about effective ways to deal with offense, open your heart to the Spirit of God so that He can help you every day of your life to die to yourself and be alive in Christ. Walk in forgiveness and love, no matter what you may go through or experience at the hands of people. People will always be people; they will always do things or say things that will not sit well with you, but you must have enough grace to forgive and not take offense.

Jesus dealt with offense or opposition in an effectual way during His ministry here on earth, and He taught His disciples to do the same. Let us learn from our Master and Teacher how we too can effectively deal with offense. In Matthew 5:38–41 Jesus stated:

> *"You have heard that it was said, An eye for an eye and a tooth for a tooth. But I tell you, don't resist an evildoer. On the contrary, if anyone slaps you on your right cheek, turn the other to him also. As for the one who wants to sue you and take away your shirt, let him have your coat as well. And if anyone forces you to go one mile, go with him two."*

What did Jesus mean when He said to "turn the other cheek" when offended or slapped on one cheek? It is important to understand what Jesus was teaching here if we are to learn how to deal with offense or persecution. First, let's look at the context of Matthew 5:38–41. In Jesus' day the legal principle was that the punishment was to fit the crime committed by an individual. For example, if a person poked out another person's eye, his or her eye was to be poked out too. It was as simple as that, and there was no mercy. It was simply a matter of "what you do to another person shall also be done to you with the same measure." Apparently, this law was made to prevent the cruel and barbaric punishments that characterized many ancient countries of that day. An "eye for an eye" was not a passport to vengeance but a law set in place to help guide the courts in determining appropriate action or punishment for the crime committed. Here are a few scriptures where we see this law of retribution taught.

> *When men get in a fight and hit a pregnant woman so that her children are born prematurely but there is no injury, the one who hit her must be fined as the woman's husband demands from him, and he must pay according to judicial assessment. If there is an injury, then you must give life for life, eye for eye, tooth for tooth, hand for hand, foot for foot, burn for burn, bruise for bruise, wound for wound.* (Exodus 21:22–25)

> *If any man inflicts a permanent injury on his neighbor, whatever he has done is to be done to him: fracture for fracture, eye for eye, tooth for tooth. Whatever injury he inflicted on the person, the same is to be inflicted on him.* (Leviticus 24:19–20)

> *You must not show pity: life for life, eye for eye, tooth for tooth, hand for hand, and foot for foot.* (Deuteronomy 19:21)

There is some debate among Bible scholars as to whether "life for life, eye for eye, tooth for tooth," and so on were to be taken literally or whether the principle was simply that the punishment must fit the crime. But what we know is that in Matthew 5:38–41 Jesus was using this teaching to raise the bar even higher by teaching a kingdom principle of "turning the other cheek" instead of retribution or revenge. Most of the times when we are wronged, our automatic or natural response is to avenge the wrong done against us so that we can prove our strength and get even. But Jesus urged His disciples not to seek vengeance. No matter how big the offense was, they were to overcome the offense with good (forgiveness) and not with evil (revenge).

Romans 12:21 says, "Do not be overcome by evil, but overcome evil with good" (NIV). When you are wronged or offended and you retaliate, it means that evil has overcome you; but when you respond by forgiving the offender (turning the other cheek), you are making a statement to the enemy that evil cannot overcome you because God's goodness and mercy resides in you and you are consumed by His love and mercy. Some people use wrongs done to them to justify their slanderous spirit against others, and many more try to cover up or excuse their ungodly attitude of revenge by saying, "I was just doing to him what he did to me or to my family." Instead, as children of God, offense should present us with an opportunity to grow spiritually and to display God's grace and love in our lives. Jesus Christ conquered opposition on the cross, not with evil, but with God's goodness when He cried out, "Father, forgive them, because they do not know what they are doing."

The apostle Peter remembered Jesus' teaching on "turning the other cheek" and encouraged his readers not to repay evil for evil or to retaliate with insults when people insulted them but instead to pay back wrongs with a blessing (1 Peter 3:9–11). Kingdom people do not live their lives by worldly standards but by the standards or principles that govern the kingdom of God; namely, forgiveness, mercy, and love. As a kingdom person, you are not to respond to offense as the world does (revenge) but by displaying God's mercy, forgiveness, and love. According to Jesus, that means you are to "turn the other cheek" when someone slaps (offends) you on the right cheek. When you respond to offense by forgiving and showing mercy, you are simply "turning the other cheek." In doing so, you overcome all the evil intentions of the Devil and conquer his tactics and gimmicks. You may look foolish in the eyes of people when you choose to forgive your offenders instead of retaliating, but to God and in the spiritual realm you are a giant, an overcomer, and a victor—and you leave room for God to act on your behalf.

In God's kingdom there is no evil, and vengeance is an unacceptable attitude, as is insulting and slandering someone or gossiping about someone, no matter how hurt you may be. Instead of reacting in vengeance toward those who hurt you, pray for them and demonstrate a kingdom lifestyle and God's strength. If you are to overcome evil and successfully deal with offense, you need to understand this principle: *You cannot stop people from speaking evil words against you or from offending you, but you can stop yourself from speaking evil words against others or offending them.* As long as you do what is right and focus on God rather than on your offenders, their assaults on you will be empty and powerless. Your duty is to keep your conduct above criticism and away from offense, and your enemies will be ashamed and come up short because the Lord is your protector, your refuge, and your dwelling place.

Don't Defend Yourself When You Are Offended—God Will Defend You

It is important to understand that "he who dwells in the shelter of the Most High will abide in the shadow of the Almighty" (Psalm 91:1 ESV). The Lord is his refuge and fortress (Psalm 91:2). That means if we are in Christ, an attack on us is an attack on God Himself, because we are hidden under His shelter. Most people retaliate when they are wronged because their ego and pride cannot accept walking in humility or going down without fighting. We are to humble ourselves and deal with offense through God's forgiveness, love, and mercy. Being in Christ and remaining in Him and allowing Him to influence our lives every moment is key to effectively dealing with offense, because when Christ is in us and we are in Him, forgiveness and love will overflow freely from our hearts.

When God's hand is upon you, no weapon or tactic of the enemy can prosper against you. When you give your life over to God, God not only blesses and receives you, but He also becomes your protector, provider, source of life, and sustenance. So when the agents of evil, through offense or opposition, try to destroy what God has done in you and intends to do through you, don't panic or go after them. Instead, sit tight in the presence and power of God through prayer, worship, and praise, and say to the enemy, "Nice try, but I am not moved or shaken by your attacks because I am protected 24/7 by the blood of Jesus Christ, and I am resurrected to live in the power and anointing of the resurrected life of Jesus Christ. I am dead to attacks because 'I no longer live, but Christ lives in me' (Galatians 2:20)."

By teaching His disciples to turn the other cheek, Jesus was clearly teaching them how to deal with offense effectively. The world thinks turning the other cheek is a sign of weakness, but in the kingdom of God, the "weak" things are the "strongest" and the "foolish" things are the "wisest" (1 Corinthians 1:27). The kingdom of God functions in a very different way and on a totally different level than does the world in which we live. The Bible strongly emphasizes this and thus tells us, "Do not conform to the pattern of this world, but be transformed by the renewing of your mind" (Romans 12:2 NIV).

Jesus Himself said to the religious people of His day, "You are from below; I am from above. You are of this world; I am not of this world" (John 8:23 NIV). In other words, their refusal to accept Jesus as the promised Messiah and the only way to the Father was due to their worldly concept of the Messiah. To operate in God, we need to think differently from the world because even though we are in this world, we are not "of the world" (John 15:19; 17:14–16). Turning the other cheek is not a sign of weakness; it is a sign of strength. As Christians we possess more power than those who have not yet given their lives over to the influence of the power of God's kingdom or those who are "religious" but are yet to experience the presence and power of God in their lives. So counterattacking such people when they offend us is really a sign of immaturity in Christ. Mature people in Christ are strong in the Lord, they exercise patience, and they are forgiving. They do not fight spiritual battles with their natural strength but with their spiritual strength through prayer. Mature people in Christ are in this world, but they are not of this world, so the culture of this world does not control them. They are humble and quick to forgive because they are controlled instead by the culture, principles, and government of God.

Jesus taught His disciples to walk in humility. When offended, they were to drop their ego and pride and not respond by taking matters into their own hands and seeking vengeance. Instead, they were to walk in the power of forgiveness, for in so doing they would defeat opposition and persecution. Even when they were killed for their faith, they would still be victors. Jesus knew that offense was a dangerous trap and a stumbling block to the disciples' faith, relationships with others, and fellowship with God. Their response to offense or persecution was critical to the advancement of the kingdom of God and having an impact upon their communities and upon this world. If they were not careful, offense would lure them away from God's mission and completely stop them from proclaiming the good news of the kingdom of God.

If we are going to live for God in a world full of hatred and offense and powerfully proclaim the life-changing gospel of Jesus Christ to the nations, we too need to walk in humility and forgiveness. As we have already stated, offense is the Devil's bait to get us into sin, to hinder us from experiencing the rule and reign of God, and to obstruct us from fulfilling our God-given mission of proclaiming the gospel of the Lord Jesus Christ to all the nations. Furthermore, offense can prevent us from having a stable relationship and fellowship with God and with other believers in Christ. Yet we can overpower offense through humility and forgiveness.

A Few Hints on Dealing with Offense

Here are some helpful hints on how you can respond to and overcome offense and opposition in your life, walk in the victorious power of God, and avoid been lured into the snare of the enemy.

1. Die to Yourself.

"My old self has been crucified with Christ. It is no longer I who live, but Christ lives in me. So I live in this earthly body by trusting in the Son of God, who loved me and gave himself for me" (Galatians 2:20 NLT).

One of the secrets of effectively dealing with offense is "dying to your old self." Your old self demands revenge. It responds to offense or opposition by counterattacking the enemy and furiously defending itself so that it doesn't appear to be weak or taken advantage of. But your "new self," or new nature in Christ, leaves or surrenders the matter into the hands of the God of justice. It does not allow offense to get hold of the heart or develop its roots in the heart but instead immediately flushes anger out through the powerful weapon of forgiveness. A dead person cannot be offended, cannot offend others, and cannot respond to offense. So if we have indeed died to ourselves through Christ's death, then we no longer live according to the desires of our fleshly bodies, which means whatever man does or says to our "fleshly body" should never be permitted to pierce through our hearts. When we are dead in Christ, it becomes easier not to respond to offense because we are alive only to the voice and Spirit of God, and nothing else matters.

2. Don't Let Pride and Ego Take Over Your Heart.
"The highway of the upright avoids evil; the one who guards his way protects his life. Pride comes before destruction, and an arrogant spirit before a fall" (Proverbs 16:17–18).

To effectively deal with offense or opposition, we must kill our pride and ego because they rise up in us to seek revenge and payback for the wrongs done to us. Pride and ego are a restless fire that can turn a small situation into a bigger one. But we must always remember that pride and ego can lead us to stumble in our walk with God and to fall away from the presence of God. We seldom realize that we naturally respond to offense or opposition out of pride and ego; hence, we say things like, "Who is he or she to say or do things like that to me?" or "Does he or she really know who I am?" If we are not careful, pride and ego can cause us to act in ways that bring about our downfall and bring shame to the name of God. *What* we are in the eyes of people is not important; *whose* we are is what is important. If we are believers, we are children of God, and because we are children of the all-powerful God, God will fight for us and defend us, so there is no need to seek revenge.

3. Turn to God in Prayer.
"Call on Me in a day of trouble; I will rescue you, and you will honor Me" (Psalm 50:15). *"Call to Me and I will answer you and tell you great and incomprehensible things you do not know"* (Jeremiah 33:3).

When you are troubled or in any difficult situation in life, do not rush anywhere else but to God through the power of prayer. God will give you wisdom to respond to offense in a manner that brings glory and honor to His name. He also can help the offending person to grow and mature in Christ or see God in you.

4. Be Slow to Speak (respond) and Slow to Become Angry.
"Understand this, my dear brothers and sisters: You must all be quick to listen, slow to speak, and slow to get angry" (James 1:19 NLT).

"Don't let your spirit rush to be angry, for anger abides in the heart of fools" (Ecclesiastes 7:9).

"A patient person shows great understanding, but a quick-tempered one promotes foolishness" (Proverbs 14:29).

When you are offended or someone says offensive words to you, do not be in a hurry to respond or let your spirit rush to be angry. Instead, look to God to comfort your troubled spirit. By so doing, you will protect both your spiritual life and the name of God, because when you respond out of the hurt and pain you have experienced, you will do or say things that should never be said or done, and you will end up regretting it. There are many people who are living in regret because of the way they responded to offense or problems in their lives. Many have lost friends and jobs because of their reaction in what we call the "heat of the moment." There are even good people (Christians included) around the world who are sitting in prisons just because they allowed "the heat of the moment" to control their emotions and pollute their hearts with evil intentions so that they responded to a situation in a deadly way. Be slow to respond so that you give the Holy Spirit an opportunity to minister to your spirit and comfort your heart.

Refrain from anger and give up your rage; do not be agitated—it can only bring harm. For evildoers will be destroyed, but those who put their hope in the LORD *will inherit the land.* (Psalm 37:8–9)

Your response to any problem in your life should never be grounded in anger but in God's strength, love, mercy, and stability. Anger brings destruction. It can destroy your future, and it can destroy God's reputation. Remember, when you are offended, just remain calm because the living God will fight for you. Every problem you encounter as a Christian should be looked at in a positive way—as a stepping-stone to spiritual growth and maturity. Offense is simply a test of your faith, stability, and maturity in God. Let it lead to growth, not destruction.

5. Be Led Always by the Holy Spirit and Not by the Flesh.
"So then, brothers, we are not obligated to the flesh to live according to the flesh, for if you live according to the flesh, you are going to die. But if by the Spirit you put to death the deeds of the body, you will live. All those led by God's Spirit are God's sons" (Romans 8:12–14).

In order for us to deal with offense in a powerful way, we need the Holy Spirit and we need Him to influence and lead us every second, minute, hour, and day of our lives. Without Him, we are nothing, and we can do nothing.

Amidst opposition, the Holy Spirit will be your strength, encouragement, and comforter. He will intercede for you, and He will help you in your weakness. Instead of responding to offense with anger, you will respond in peace and allow the Holy Spirit to minister to your hurting soul and fill you with the love of God for your enemy. Through Him you will demonstrate the love of God, and He will empower you to seek peace and walk in it.

How Can We Avoid Offending Others?
Here are three effective ways you can avoid causing others to stumble in their faith and walk with God: (1) By being in Christ at all times; (2) by being a doer of the Word of God and not just a hearer; and (3) by walking in the power of the Holy Spirit and not by the influence of your flesh. Your old self (flesh) demands revenge, but your new life in Christ commands you to walk in the power of the Spirit so that you do not

fulfil the demands of your old self (flesh). The flesh is hostile to peace, forgiveness, love, and mercy because it is hostile to the God of peace, love, forgiveness, and mercy. God calls us to walk in the power of His Spirit so that we can display and walk in the fruit of His Spirit (Galatians 5:22–23). When you walk according to the power of the Holy Spirit, you will speak from the heart of God—from the wisdom and life of His Word—and not from the depth of your own hurts or feelings.

Living our lives according to our flesh is extremely dangerous and costly. When the flesh is dominant in our lives, pride, arrogance, anger, and ungodliness take over, which makes it very easy for us to be offended and to respond to offense in wicked and harmful ways. Where there is pride and arrogance, there are no restraints on doing evil. However, people who are full of God and His Word are full of the Holy Spirit. And when people are full of the Holy Spirit, they are considerate, slow to anger, forgiving, loving, inclusive peacemakers, and they are difficult to offend because they are not focused on themselves or their feelings but on God and the fulfillment of His will here on earth. If we want to make an impact on this world and bring transformation, we must walk and live in the power of the Holy Spirit, and we must desire to remove from our lives any and every stumbling block to fulfilling that mission. Unforgiveness, pride, offense, hatred, bitterness, and anger are stumbling blocks to the mission and calling of God upon our lives, to our unity and stability, and to our breakthrough in life. When we take all these things out of our lives, we will excel and do extraordinary things for the kingdom of God.

Remove Every Stumbling Block in Your Life

In His mission to rescue humankind from the power of sin and death, Jesus did not allow anything to be a stumbling block to Him. Not even forty days of Satan's temptation in the wilderness could succeed in taking Him away from His God-given goal of rescuing and recovering humankind from the kingdom of darkness and bringing them into the kingdom of light. Neither did He allow Peter's "rebuke" to derail His mission and purpose here on earth (Matthew 16:23). When Jesus told Peter, "Get behind Me, Satan!" He was not saying Peter was literally

"Satan," of course, but Peter's attempt to convince Jesus to evade His mission, which required His death on the cross, was a stumbling block and the Devil's weapon to discourage Jesus from fulfilling His mission.

There are many things in our lives that are stumbling blocks to our relationship and fellowship with God, to our success in life, to our callings and gifts, and to our future in God—things such as bad friends (influence), bad relationships, pride, and unforgiveness, just to mention a few. If we do not command these things to "get behind us," we will never progress spiritually from one level to another.

If you don't know why your life is stuck or things don't seem to work out or go your way, I suggest you check the contents and condition of your heart before you start casting out all the devils. Bitterness, offense, unforgiveness, or bad company may be stopping you from moving forward in life, and the only weapon that can overcome these is the weapon of forgiveness. When you forgive, you clear away all the stumbling blocks from your life, and God illuminates your path so that you can grow spiritually and move from one level in life to another without any hindrances. You can be a powerful man or woman of God, but only if you deal with the stumbling blocks in your life through forgiveness.

Offense gives birth to unforgiveness if it is not dealt with properly, and when the spirit of unforgiveness takes over your life, God's Spirit in you becomes polluted or contaminated, which means anything you do or say will have a toxic nature. It is important to know that the spirit behind what you do or say is more important than your actions because you can do the right thing but with the wrong motive. So don't let offense or any of the toxic things we have already mentioned corrupt the good character and nature of God in you. Walk in humility, forgiveness, and mercy and in God's love, and do not be easily offended so that you can fulfill your potential in life and walk in the power and anointing of God.

Just as our Master, Jesus, did not allow offense to lure Him away from His purpose and important mission here on earth, we must follow in His footsteps and not allow anything to lure us away from God's purpose for our life. Jesus did not give in to the Devil's demands. He walked in humility and according to the kingdom of God, not according to the world. He understood that He was in the world but not of the world (John 18:36). The same is true of us who are born of the Spirit of God—we are in this world but not of this world (John 17:16). We belong to the kingdom of God, and our citizenship is in heaven (Philippians 3:20–21). Offense will come our way because we are not of this world. God has chosen us out of this world, and because of that the world hates us (John 15:19), and Satan will do anything and everything to try to offend us so that he can pull us away from living in the power of God.

Now that we have a clear picture and understanding of what offense is and how we can deal with it, in the next chapter we are going to look in greater depth at the evil of unforgiveness and how it gives birth to hatred and jealousy and how jealousy leads to ungodly actions. As we transition to that chapter, it is important to understand that living a life full of unforgiveness is dangerous. It is a time bomb that can explode any minute and shut down our life, career, and God's calling upon our life. Unforgiveness is a huge hindrance to the power of God moving in our life to use us mightily.

Chapter 6

THE DANGERS OF UNFORGIVENESS

Hatred and Jealousy

IN ORDER TO UNDERSTAND MORE FULLY THE DANGERS OF UNFORGIVENESS AND HOW IT leads people into evil actions and away from the Spirit and presence of God, we are going to look at some biblical accounts that illustrate these points. Our goal in this chapter is to learn to forgive people quickly and not allow the spirit of anger to rule over our lives. Unforgiveness cultivates a spirit of jealousy and hatred, and when a heart is filled with hatred and jealousy, evil actions are inevitable. If we are to avoid a life of anger, bitterness, and brokenheartedness, which stifle the power of God, it is important to know the tactics of the enemy. The enemy's primary tactic is to use offense and unforgiveness to keep us away from the power of God and away from His vision for our lives.

In Genesis 27 we find the interesting account of Isaac and his two sons, Esau and Jacob. Isaac, the great man of God, was now about one hundred years old (see Genesis 25:26 and 26:34), and his eyes were so weak he could not see. Knowing his days were numbered, he called for his older son Esau and said to him, "Look, I am old and do not know the day of my death. Take your hunting gear, your quiver and bow, and go out in the field to hunt some game for me. Then make me a delicious meal that I love and bring it to me to eat, so that I can bless you before I die" (Genesis 27:2–4). Now, Rebekah, Isaac's wife, was nearby, listening to Isaac's conversation with his oldest son.

Now, what is so fascinating in this account is that when Rebekah learned about Isaac's plan to bless Esau, she quickly devised a plan to trick her husband into blessing their younger son, Jacob, instead. But why? It is true that Rebekah favored Jacob over Esau (Genesis 25:28), but she also remembered the Lord's words from many years before about Jacob dominating his older brother. The Lord had said to her in Genesis 25:23, "Two nations are in your womb; two people will come from you and be separated. One people will be stronger than the other, and the older will serve the younger." In the ancient Eastern tradition, the oldest son was the rightful person to inherit his father's blessings. However, acting on a decades-old prophecy about Jacob dominating his older brother, Rebekah found a way to overturn that and let their younger son, Jacob, receive the blessings, as prophesied by the Lord.

So Rebekah managed to trick Isaac into blessing Jacob instead of Esau. But note this: Earlier in Genesis 25:30–34, Jacob tricked his older brother into selling his birthright to him for some food. This was not a coincidence but by design to fulfill what was going to take place in the life of Jacob as prophesied by the Lord. Yes, Jacob was a trickster and Rebekah a liar, to put it plainly, but what we need to understand in this account is that God can achieve His purposes and plans and promises whatever the situation or circumstances might be. As for the circumstances, Jacob was "outside" the realm of receiving his father's blessing because he was younger than Esau and did not have the birthright, but because of his love for meat, Esau willingly sold his birthright to Jacob, which put Jacob into the position of the older son who would receive the blessing of his father.

The birthright was the right of a firstborn son to receive a double portion (in this case, two-thirds) of the inheritance from his father (Deuteronomy 21:17). I am not suggesting here that deceiving people in order to get what you want in life is permissible. There are consequences to deceit, and Jacob was not spared from the repercussions of his deceitfulness. He too was deceived by his uncle, Laban, his family was torn apart by strife, and he was exiled from his family for years. Furthermore, God could have fulfilled His plan for Jacob in His own way and at His own time without the help of Rebekah and Jacob. But it is what it is; Jacob got the blessings instead of his older brother. This caused Esau to be filled with anger and jealousy toward his younger brother, Jacob.

Anger, Hatred, and Jealousy = Murder

Esau reacted in anger and declared, "The days of mourning for my father are approaching; then I will kill my brother Jacob" (Genesis 27:41). Esau's anger made him forget his own fault in selling his "birthright" to his younger brother for just a bowl of stew. Hatred built up in his heart to the point that all he wanted to do was kill his younger brother. Esau was right to be angry and upset at Jacob after he was cheated out of his blessings, but he wasn't right to stay angry. What Rebekah and Jacob did was wrong, but it didn't give Esau the right to murder his brother. Instead, Esau should have forgiven his younger brother and left the matter in the hands of God—the God of justice.

Esau's reaction to Jacob being blessed and to the offense of being tricked is the focal point in this gripping and compelling account. Esau's determination to retaliate teaches us a lot, and very few people have focused on it. His reaction paints a colorful picture of how offense can produce anger, hatred, and jealousy and can cause a person to act in the most evil way possible. In most cases when we are wronged or others conspire against us, anger is the first and most natural reaction. But anger is not a problem or sin in itself. The problem arises when we allow anger to sink into our hearts and grow into bitterness, hatred, and jealousy. And when bitterness, hatred, and jealousy are fully grown and developed in a person's heart, the desire to seek vengeance or cause harm increases. Hateful people are jealous, and jealous people are eager to cause harm, physically, mentally, or verbally.

The remedy for anger is forgiveness, not anger management. Anger management helps people to "hold" their anger in, while forgiveness helps people to release their anger and let go of it. Many people who have been through anger management are more likely to get angry because the tension of the hurt is still there, while people who forgive their enemies are less likely to be angry and more likely to walk in love and show mercy and grace to the offender.

As Christians and God-fearing people, we must understand that no wrong ever justifies killing another person or acting in an ungodly way toward someone. In the spiritual world, killing a person takes different forms and is not restricted to physical murder. Each time we gossip, slander, hate or show hatred toward a person, give a false report about a person, or despise someone, we are committing murder. We have the right to be angry and upset when we are wronged, but wrong done against us does not justify or give us permission to gossip, slander, and assassinate someone's character. When you are wronged, instead of reacting in anger, respond by forgiving, praying, and allowing the Holy Spirit to take full charge of your situation.

We are called to forgive and let God act on our behalf. Romans 12:19–21 says this:

> *Friends, do not avenge yourselves; instead, leave room for His wrath. For it is written: Vengeance belongs to Me; I will repay, says the Lord. But "If your enemy is hungry, feed him. If he is thirsty, give him something to drink. For in so doing you will be heaping fiery coals on his head." Do not be conquered by evil, but conquer evil with good.*

Instead of responding in anger to your enemy, respond in the power of forgiveness and love. Only a person who has forgiven can love and feed his or her enemy or give that enemy a drink. Unforgiveness can lead you to seek revenge through your own strength, and that always results in a big defeat. Unforgiveness also can trap you in the spirit of hatred and jealousy toward other people. Sadly, many people are jealous of others because of the spirit of hatred and unforgiveness.

Jealousy Produces Hatred

In Genesis 4 we read the account of Abel and Cain. Abel was a shepherd of flocks, while Cain worked the ground. In the course of time, Cain presented some of the land's produce to the Lord as an offering, and Abel also presented an offering of some of the firstborn of his flock and their fat portions. What is intriguing is that the Lord had regard for Abel and his offering but did not have regard for Cain and his offering. We are not told why God did not accept Cain's offering, but from Cain's reaction after the Lord did not consider his offering, it seems apparent God did not accept Cain's offering because He saw an ungodly attitude in his heart.

To God, the spirit and attitude behind what we do for Him is far more important than what we do outwardly for Him. In the kingdom of God, motives and attitudes matter greatly. Because of this truth, it is safe to say that Cain's attitude or motive behind his gift to the Lord was wrong. Proverbs 21:27 says, "The sacrifice of an evil person is detestable, especially when it is offered with wrong motives" (NLT).

Let's look again at Cain's reaction for a moment, because this will give us a fresh picture of what the spirit of jealousy and hatred can cause a person to do. When the Lord refused to acknowledge Cain's gift, Cain responded by being furious and extremely angry. He looked despondent, and the Lord said to him, "Why are you furious? And why do you look despondent? If you do what is right, won't you be accepted? But if you do not do what is right, sin is crouching at the door. Its desire is for you, but you must rule over it" (Genesis 4:6–7). Cain was very angry because the Lord accepted Abel's sacrifice. Instantly, the spirit of jealousy toward Abel kicked in, and it eventually produced hatred. Even the warning from the Lord and His encouragement to Cain to do what was right and not give in to sin did not stop the fire of jealousy and hatred in Cain's heart. Cain failed to control his anger, and consequently he opened himself up to the "evil spirit" of jealousy and hatred. The end result was his murder of his brother.

When people see others being blessed by God or doing well in life or in ministry, they often respond with anger and envy, but little do they know they are opening themselves up to the influence and power of hatred and jealousy. They slowly start to discredit and tarnish the other person's character and try to stop everything God intends to do through that person. Many people today have had their future and dreams dismantled by others because of the spirit of hatred and jealousy. Countless marriages have been torn apart and gifts in the body of Christ have been silenced because of slander and gossip. We need to clearly understand that this is the gimmick of Satan to stop the momentum of the kingdom of God on the earth. Those who participate in gossip, slander, or discrediting other Christians help the enemy to fulfill his plans. In other words, they become ministers of evil.

Many people have hatred (a deep, emotional, extreme dislike) of others simply because of the spirit of unforgiveness, so they gossip as a response to the hurts they harbor in their hearts. Hatred can be uprooted only by the power of the Holy Spirit through forgiveness. Forgiving those who have wronged you can surely preserve your life and your future in Christ and their lives and futures too. Furthermore, through forgiveness you avoid reacting in a costly manner. Prisons around the world are full of people who committed murder or other crimes due to hatred and jealousy. Everything you desire to do for God must be done without the spirit of jealousy, because jealousy causes you to focus on people and what God is doing in them, instead of focusing on God and what He desires to do in and through you. When you see others enjoying the favor of God, praise God and celebrate with them, and let their blessings inspire and motivate you to remain in God and do what is right in the eyes of God—and God will bless you.

Another biblical account that illustrates the dangers of unforgiveness, hatred, and jealousy is that of Joseph in Genesis 37. We are told in verses 3–5 that Israel (Jacob) loved Joseph more than his other sons because Joseph was born to him in his old age, and he made a special robe for Joseph. When his brothers saw that their father loved Joseph more than all of them, they hated Joseph and could not bring themselves to speak peaceably to him. The situation grew even worse when Joseph had dreams that he shared with his brothers. According to Joseph's dreams, Joseph was going to reign over his brothers, and this fueled their hatred even more. Joseph may have been immature and naïve to share such dreams with his brothers, but his brothers had no right to react the way they did—with anger, hatred, jealousy, and a desire to harm him. They decided at first to kill Joseph, but in the end they resolved to sell him as a slave to the Ishmaelites for twenty pieces of silver.

Now look at Genesis 37:23–24. Before they sold Joseph into slavery, his brothers stripped him of his robe (his dignity, credibility, and anointing), and they threw him into the pit (discrediting, dishonoring, and disgracing him) so they could stop Joseph from emerging as their leader, as his dreams indicated. Joseph's brothers' jealousy gave birth to an ugly rage that blinded them from doing what was right. They couldn't forgive him or get over their anger, and as a result, all they wanted was to kill their younger brother. Such is the evil of unforgiveness.

Joseph's brothers' reaction is very similar to the reaction we see from some ungodly people when they see someone doing well or enjoying the Lord's favor. They try to destroy that person's dignity and credibility through gossip or slander. They question God's anointing upon that person's life. And then they move on to throw such a person into a "pit" through defamation of character, trying to discredit all the Lord is doing through that person. Before we even realize what is happening, God's calling upon that person and his or her reputation in society has been badly bruised and tarnished. Jealousy is an agent of evil that tries to stop the work of God and hinder people from stepping into their destiny. Joseph's brothers had a jealous spirit, and they tried to stop Joseph from stepping into his destiny, but God's purpose and plans for Joseph could not be thwarted.

Joseph's Heart of Forgiveness

The greatest lesson we learn from the story of Joseph comes from the gracious, merciful, and forgiving response of Joseph to his brothers. When severe famine came upon the land, Jacob told his sons to go to Egypt to buy grain (Genesis 42), but little could Jacob's sons have imagined that Joseph, the brother they had sold into slavery, was going to be their savior from hunger. When Joseph's brothers came to Egypt looking for food, Joseph, who was now the prime minister, could have retaliated and punished them for what they had done to him. Instead, Joseph chose to demonstrate the character and nature of God by forgiving them and giving them food.

The natural response of any human being in Joseph's place would be to seek revenge or boast, "I told you I was going to rule over you." But Joseph was humble. He used his authority, not to harm his brothers, but instead to sustain their lives by blessing them with food. When you don't allow offense to influence you, bitterness, hatred, and anger will have no influence upon you. Furthermore, the spirit of unforgiveness will never exist in you, because where there is forgiveness, unforgiveness has no power. By blessing his brothers with food, Joseph illustrated what true forgiveness looks like.

True forgiveness reaches out, shows mercy and grace, restores, and does not remember past mistakes or offenses. We are to emulate the heart of Joseph and be a people who walk in mercy and use the weapon of forgiveness to sustain life and be a blessing to our enemies. We are also to be quick to clear any bitterness from our hearts; otherwise, we give room to the spirit of unforgiveness to rule over us. Furthermore, we must be a people who walk in love and not in hatred—regardless of what we might be going through in life. Hatred and unforgiveness lead us away from the presence of God and into the spirit of jealousy.

A Sinful Jealousy

It is important to understand that jealousy is a manifestation of the influence of Lucifer. God discharged Lucifer of his duties in heaven because he became envious of God's position as the creator of all things. It was because of jealousy that Lucifer said to himself, "I will ascend to the heavens; I will set up my throne above the stars of God. I will sit on the mount of the gods' assembly, in the remotest parts of the North. I will ascend above the highest clouds; I will make myself like the Most High" (Isaiah 14:13–14). But God sent him packing from the heavens because God does not share His glory with anybody. Angels and humans were created to glorify Him, not themselves.

It is also important to point out here that when the Bible says God is a jealous God, it doesn't mean He is envious of what we have. After all, He created us, and everything we have belongs to Him. Exodus 20:5 says, "You must not bow down to [idols] or worship them; for I, the LORD your God, am a jealous God." There, however, the word *jealous* does not speak of the *sin* of jealousy, such as being envious of someone else's position or property. Rather, it speaks of God's jealousy over a person giving the glory and honor that is His to a breathless and powerless idol. All worship, honor, and glory belong only to God, the creator of the universe, so to worship something God created provokes Him to jealousy. The only time you are allowed, or have the right, to be jealous is when someone is flirting with your spouse, because only you have the right to flirt with your spouse. This kind of jealousy is not sinful because you have the right to be jealous of someone God has rightfully given to you or placed under your care.

Sinful jealousy is when you desire something that doesn't belong to you but rightfully belongs to someone else, such as being envious of another person's gifts, skills, abilities, or position in ministry. This kind of envy is dangerous because it can lead a person to kill another person for what belongs to that person or to bring conflicts into the family of believers. According to James 4:1–2, the source of wars and fights among us is the cravings that are at war within us. These cravings make us envy one another and desire to have what someone else has so that we seek to "murder" the person who has it, either physically or through slander. As followers of Christ and ambassadors of the kingdom of God, we must resist the evil influence of jealousy, pride, and selfish ambition if we are to expand the kingdom of God here on the earth.

God has anointed each one of us with a portion of His grace and given us skills, talents, and gifts, according to our callings, so that we can function within the power and ability given to us to the glory of His holy name. Thus, when we see others operating in a different gift than ours, we must never feel intimidated or worthless because every gift is extremely important in the body of Christ. Your gift or area of grace in ministry is a tool the body of Christ needs in order to function powerfully and accomplish its mission here on earth. Rejoice with, encourage, and lift up other people as they serve the Lord with their gifts, and never be jealous of their calling. If you have a grudge against anybody, forgive that person so that you can avoid the spirit of unforgiveness, which gives birth to jealousy and hatred.

Hatred is never acceptable. In fact, the Bible declares that a hateful person is not born of God, but of the Devil:

- "A hateful person disguises himself with his speech and harbors deceit within" (Proverbs 26:24).
- "Everyone who hates his brother is a murderer, and you know that no murderer has eternal life residing in him" (1 John 3:15).

- "Anyone who claims to be in the light but hates a brother or sister is still in the darkness" (1 John 2:9 NIV).
- "But anyone who hates a brother or sister is in the darkness and walks around in the darkness. They do not know where they are going, because the darkness has blinded them" (1 John 2:11 NIV).

The Impact of Unforgiveness

While it has been said repeatedly already, it is crucial to understand that unforgiveness is a dangerous spirit that can have a negative impact upon a person's life, both physically and spiritually. Many people today are not walking in the power of God or seeing open doors in their lives because of the spirit of unforgiveness. Furthermore, it is because of the spirit of unforgiveness in the body of Christ that the fire of God has been quenched and very few miracles are being experienced. Unforgiveness is a sin, and where there is sin, God's presence and anointing are absent. The Lord's hand is not too short to save or to do mighty things here on earth and in our lives, and His ear is not too deaf to hear our cry for His intervention in the world; however, our lack of forgiveness has built barriers between God and us. Moreover, it also has created a barricade between us and other believers in Christ. Consequently, we can't receive from each other or minister powerfully to each other, and we can't even hear the voice of God. If we are ever to see real reformation and revival in our generation, we must forgive those who have wronged us so that the Spirit of God can operate in us freely and without any hindrance.

Forgiveness is powerful because it creates an atmosphere for the Holy Spirit of God and His power to move and do what He does best—transform lives, revive dead or cold souls, generate peace, and empower God's people to do the will of God. If you want to have a breakthrough in life, live a stress-free life, and experience the real power of God and walk in His presence, here are some keys:

- Turn your resentment, jealousy, and hatred over to God.
- Pray for those who persecute or willfully offend you.
- Don't take matters into your own hands or repay evil for evil.

- Don't take things too personally; if you do, Satan will pounce on you.
- Rejoice with others when they are being blessed.
- Be quick to apologize and to maintain peace.
- Walk in humility (humility is not a weakness but a strength of God in you).
- Finally, forgive, no matter what the circumstances might be. Forgiveness restores your fellowship and relationship, not only with the offender, but also with God. Furthermore, it restores your spiritual position in the kingdom of God.

Personally, when I have followed these principles or keys, I have seen and experienced some interesting and miraculous things in my life and ministry. God has been able to open new doors for me; I have had financial breakthroughs, spiritual growth, spiritual maturity, and an increase in my passion and zeal for the kingdom of God and for winning souls for Jesus Christ. Above all, my motive for doing what God has called me to do has been cleansed so that I do not do things to prove wrong those who oppose or offend me. I live without stress, disappointment, or feelings of bitterness but with the joy and peace of the Lord. Because of this, I live for one purpose and one purpose only: To please my God and fulfill His calling upon my life to help many people come to know Christ and have their lives transformed and sanctified through His blood.

When you have forgiven all your offenders and released all the toxin of unforgiveness, the Devil has no power over you or attachment to you. He can never bring you down because you walk in the spirit of forgiveness and have your life rooted in God and His Word, so that you stand firm against any tactics of the enemy (Proverbs 12:3). An unforgiving person has no roots in God, so he or she crumbles in times of opposition. If you walk in forgiveness and forgive those who have taken advantage of you and hurt you, you will see the hand of God work mightily in your life and turn to good what the enemy meant for evil. Above all, God will bring your enemies to their knees, and they will confess and repent of their wrongs and mend their relationship with you so that God's work on the earth can peacefully and powerfully advance.

Finally, unforgiveness is a danger to the church and to the activity of God because it creates an atmosphere of fierce competition between churches, ministries, and Christians. This is why there is so much disunity in the body of Christ today. People want to prove others wrong by showing off how powerful they are through their talents or callings. How shameful! We are not called to compete with each other but to work together in unity as one body to fulfill the will of God on the earth. We may have different gifts, talents, or callings, but these all come from the same God, our Creator and the Father of all humanity. To compete with each other is not only a shame but also a disgrace; it is inspired by the spirit of witchcraft. How can the hands compete with the head, or the head with the legs, or the ears with the eyes (cf. 1 Corinthians 12:12-31)? The Holy Spirit is not in competition with Jesus Christ, and Jesus Christ is not in competition with God the Father. The three are a united force that work together to accomplish the mission of the kingdom of God.

One of the main causes of competition in the body of Christ, or in any relationship, is the spirit of jealousy, covetousness, and envy, which springs up into full-blown division, strife, and hatred. We can eliminate the spirit of competition in our lives by first eliminating the spirit of unforgiveness and hatred. Hatred and unforgiveness create a spirit of competition, while forgiveness and walking in love inspire unity in the body of Christ or in any relationship. Proverbs 10:12 says, "Hatred stirs up conflicts, but love covers all offenses." Loving people, unlike those who are full of hatred, are willing to put up with offense and slander and to forgive those who wrong them.

Unforgiveness is dangerous because it leaves a person open to Satan's attacks. Many people who are behind bars are not bad people or evil people. They simply opened themselves up to the enemy's attacks and influence because of unforgiveness. Don't let unforgiveness rob you of your destiny in God or influence you to do ungodly things. Forgive those who have wronged you, and surrender to God whatever hurts you might have in your heart so that you can walk in peace and freedom.

Use Your Tongue to Unleash the Love of God upon People

Use the power of your tongue to unleash the weapon of forgiveness upon the enemy's camp and the love of God upon His people. Matthew 18:18 says that we have the power to bind anything on earth and it shall be bound in heaven, or to loose anything on earth and it shall be loosed in heaven. Declare this very moment, "I loose forgiveness and mercy upon my offenders, and I bind the power and influence of an unforgiving spirit. I unleash the love of God and the power of His Word upon my heart and destroy every tactic of Satan in Jesus' name! I unleash mercy, grace, and forgiveness upon my life, the church, and my nation, and I bind every plan of the enemy to cause division and confusion in our midst. In the power of Jesus' name, amen!"

Chapter 7

THE WEAPON OF FORGIVENESS

Satan Can't Stand it

THE POWER OF FORGIVENESS IS VERY UNDERESTIMATED AND MISUNDERSTOOD. IN FACT, TO a person with a worldly mind-set, it is almost impossible to comprehend and is considered foolishness. In the world today, forgiving someone or asking for forgiveness is viewed as a weakness. Because of this negative and deadly view of forgiveness, many people find it difficult to effectively forgive or ask for forgiveness. There is even a deception that has emerged over the years in the Christian world that a few ministers are teaching; namely, that we don't need to repent or ask for forgiveness when we sin against God. Their argument is that God has already forgiven our sins. What a deadly and deceptive teaching this is! If we could only grasp the powerful work repentance and forgiveness does in our relationship and fellowship with God and in the spiritual realm, we would never fall for this error. Asking God for forgiveness and repenting of our sins goes deeper than just admitting our sins. It repositions us into our kingdom authority and reestablishes God's will and power upon our lives.

Yes, God has already provided forgiveness for our sins through the blood of Jesus Christ, but we must be willing to receive it by repenting of our sins and asking God for forgiveness. When that is done, a consuming fire sweeps over our heart, burns the chaff, and clears away the guilt and power of condemnation. Furthermore, Christ's forgiveness of our sins empowers us to live a restored, transformed, and new life in Him, and it never gives us a license to continue living in sin.

Just because forgiveness has been made available to all humanity does not mean we all have been forgiven of our sins. We still have to accept God's provision of forgiveness by accepting the Lord Jesus Christ in our lives and allowing Him to rule and reign in us. Forgiveness has been provided, and Christ has paid for all our sins, but we still have to take a step forward and willingly reach out to God and accept forgiveness so that we can experience His transforming presence to live a kingdom lifestyle.

In this chapter we are going to focus in greater detail on the power of forgiveness and how forgiveness is indeed a weapon Satan cannot withstand. You have learned that your forgiveness releases your offender from the "prison" of unforgiveness. That is right and true, but forgiveness goes deeper than that. The person forgiveness really releases from the snare of the Devil is you (the offended person). Forgiveness has a greater impact on you as an individual than it does on your offender. Your offender benefits greatly when you forgive him or her, but you benefit a hundred times more when you forgive. This is why forgiveness is so very important in the kingdom of God.

In our previous chapters, we have looked at what forgiveness is and its mysterious powers. We also looked at the dangers of not forgiving. Now we are going to learn how we can use the power of forgiveness as a weapon against every scheme of the kingdom of darkness.

It is vital we understand that before we can use any other spiritual weaponry such as praise and worship or prayer, we first must use the weapon of forgiveness to dismantle every hindrance or stumbling block that may prevent us from entering the throne room of God. Many of our prayers go unanswered because of things in our lives that hinder our communication with God—anger, bitterness, hatred, and unforgiveness being prime examples. For this reason, Jesus said in Matthew 5:23–24 that when we are presenting our offering or sacrifice to God (in our day, tithes, praise and worship, prayer requests) at the altar and there we remember that somebody (friend or Christian brother or sister) has something against us, we are to leave our offering at the altar and reconcile with that person first and then come back and present our offering to God.

Many of us do not take this scripture very seriously when we come before the presence of God at a Sunday service or any time when we come into His presence to offer Him our sacrifice or ask Him to act on our behalf or move in our lives. We carelessly approach God, knowing very well that we have offended someone or we have been offended and have not forgiven our offenders. This is why we do not receive what we would like to receive from God. God's principles are straightforward and designed to work on our behalf when they are followed. If there is unforgiveness in our heart, we can pray, praise God, and worship Him outwardly all we want, but we will not receive what we ask of Him. The spirit of unforgiveness hinders us from experiencing the power and breakthrough of God in our lives. In the spiritual realm, victory begins with the power of forgiveness and things like restoration follow. If we cannot forgive our offenders, we might as well say good-bye to our breakthrough or victory.

To dig deeper into this subject, let us take a closer look at the heart of God's forgiveness of our sins. Have you ever sat down and asked yourself the following questions: Why would God choose to forgive our sins after Adam and Eve had sinned against Him? Why didn't He just destroy humanity and end His plans of placing us here on earth? Why would He sacrifice His only beloved Son, Jesus Christ, to pay for humanity's sins, which He had nothing to do with in the first place? Why would Jesus Christ die an undignified death for someone else's sins? Was there anything man could have done after the fall to earn God's forgiveness and regain his position in the kingdom of God? And finally, why would God do everything He could to redeem humanity from the power of sin and death?

Understanding the reason or motive behind God's sacrifice of His innocent and sinless Son to restore people to their place in the kingdom of God will help us unlock the power of forgiveness as a weapon the kingdom of darkness cannot and will never withstand. In Genesis 3 we read about the temptation and the fall of humanity through the deception of Satan. God had a plan and a purpose for people when He created them. His original plan was for them to bring honor, glory, and praise to His precious name by worshiping Him alone in holiness as the only true and living God. Satan, in jealousy, embarked on a journey to destroy God's original plan for humanity because he wanted to be worshiped instead of God. So he engineered the fall and contamination of human beings through sin. Sin is an offense to God, and nothing of a sinful nature is allowed to dwell in God's holy presence; hence, Adam and Eve were banished from God's presence (Genesis 3:23–24).

Adam and Eve had no way back into the presence of God because of sin, and there was nothing they could do in their own strength or power to regain their lost position and authority in God's kingdom. Satan thought he had destroyed God's plans, but Genesis 3:21 records a very important act and a sign of God's future restoration of mankind to His original intention and purpose. "The Lord God made clothing out of skins for Adam and his wife, and He clothed them." By making clothes out of skin and clothing Adam and Eve, God demonstrated His grace and forgiveness and thus started the process of redeeming humanity from the kingdom of darkness. God's use of animal skins to cover Adam and Eve anticipated the Old Testament system of animal sacrifices (cf. Leviticus 1, 3–7; Numbers 15:1–31). Through the sacrifice of an unblemished lamb (Jesus Christ), human beings would receive forgiveness of sin and consequently be readmitted into the holy presence of God.

There is one very important thing we see in God's method of redeeming mankind from the power of Satan. When Satan engineered the fall of man, God did not send out an army of His heavenly angels to physically fight Satan toe to toe. Satan was not on the same level as God almighty! All God did to defeat Satan was to use the weapon of forgiveness to easily defeat Satan's plans. To this day any sinner who turns to God and believes in the saving name of Jesus Christ is forgiven, and the power of sin and death has no hold on that person. Through God's forgiveness of our sins by means of the precious blood of Jesus Christ, we have been freed from the slavery and bondage of sin and declared righteous before God.

Satan thought he had managed to hijack God's plans, but God used the weapon of forgiveness and love to forgive the sins of His created people. God is gracious, merciful, and loving, and this is seen in His forgiving nature, or heart. We all deserve to be punished for our sins, but the blood of Jesus has taken care of our sins and our relationship and fellowship with God has been restored. We don't need to struggle or wrestle with Satan physically because the battle is not a physical battle. The battle is a spiritual battle, and Christ has already fought and won that battle on our behalf against the kingdom of darkness. All we need is to get hold of God's spiritual weapons and know how to use them. If we don't have Christ and His presence in our lives, or don't know how to use the weapons of God, we will be defeated. Religion alone will not help us win a spiritual battle. We must get hold of God's power and remain in His presence. Then we shall live a victorious Christian life. God's forgiveness of our sins has not only restored us to the kingdom of God but also has reestablished our kingdom authority and power.

No one can claim to have done something good that has secured forgiveness and salvation from God. There is, in fact, nothing we can do to make God love us more than He already does. By sacrificing His only Son, the sinless Lord Jesus Christ, God has proved to humanity His unconditional and unmatched love. The only thing we need to do on our side is to have faith in His Son, Jesus Christ. It is because of His grace and love that God sent His only begotten Son into the world to die for our sins so that everyone who believes in Him should not perish but have everlasting life (John 3:16). God has already won the battle with Satan. We simply must believe, or have faith, in Jesus Christ, and—boom!—we are saved. It is pretty simple, yet the world has a tough time comprehending the things of God, especially the means of salvation. The apostle Paul wrote in 1 Corinthians 2:14, "The unbeliever does not welcome what comes from God's Spirit, because it is foolishness to him; he is not able to understand it since it is evaluated spiritually."

God's spiritual victory through the death and resurrection of His Son, Jesus Christ, has much to teach us concerning spiritual battles. Spiritual battles must be fought with spiritual weapons, not physical weapons. When sin entered the world through Adam and Eve, the battle became a spiritual battle and not a physical one. A person can try all sorts of things in the physical realm to thwart his or her sin nature, but there will be no success. Cutting off certain TV programs will not keep someone from committing sin because sin is not a physical problem. It is a spiritual problem that needs the spiritual weapon of the blood of Jesus Christ to defeat it. Many people have failed to win battles in their lives simply because they did not grasp the nature of those battles. Even Peter, the man who spent so much time with the all-powerful Jesus, had trouble understanding that Jesus came to win a spiritual battle.

Jesus Forgave—to Defeat Satan

When the soldiers came to the garden to arrest Jesus, Peter drew his sword and struck the high priest's servant, cutting off his right ear. But Jesus commanded Peter to put his sword away. Then He touched the servant's ear and healed him (Luke 22:50–51). Thus, even at His arrest, Jesus demonstrated God's heart of forgiveness and mercy. If He had responded to the offense of the arrest as most people would, Jesus would have ignored the servant's severed ear, but because of His forgiving heart, mercy, and compassion, He healed him. Wow! In addition, if Jesus had come to fight a physical battle, He could have called upon His Father God to provide Him at once with more than twelve legions of angels to prevent His arrest and kill all those powerless soldiers (Matthew 26:53). He did not do this because the battle was spiritual, and in the spiritual realm, Jesus had already won the battle through prayer, long before the soldiers even showed up to arrest Him and while Peter and the other disciples were fast asleep. The Bible tells us that Jesus had prayed fervently and His sweat became like great drops of blood (Luke 22:44).

In His earthly ministry, Jesus won the battle against demons and sickness by using the weapon of forgiveness. And just as God the Father began by forgiving Adam and Eve when He clothed them with animal skins, at the cross, even while in excruciating pain, Jesus also forgave His tormentors, as well as the thief who was crucified alongside Him, again demonstrating how spiritual battles are to be fought and won. Here is what we need to know: Through forgiveness Jesus gave us a blueprint for how to defeat every tactic of the enemy. Forgiveness is still the power of God and a weapon that destroys every demonic plan.

Spiritual battles require spiritual weapons. Forgiveness should be the first weapon you send forth into the spiritual realms to clear the way and remove all the resistant spirits. Then when you pray, your prayers will be like lightning that strikes every demonic force and burns every ungodly spirit. And you will see miracles, healings, and signs and wonders as you pray and minister to people. If you learn to forgive, you will submit to the power of God and His anointing to accomplish His work in you and through you. This is the wonder of forgiveness. Forgive your offenders, and you will experience God's healing, life, restoration, renewal, and revival. Let go of your bitterness, hatred, and anger, and watch God miraculously begin to open all the locked doors in your life without your even fighting to open them. Forgive so that you can enjoy the peace of God and be an ambassador of His peace. When you forgive your enemies, things begin to shift in the spiritual realm, and God begins to shake every corrupt seed of bitterness, hatred, and anger out of your heart.

Notice that before He healed a paralyzed man, Jesus forgave his sins (Matthew 9:2–8). Why? Jesus knew that where there is forgiveness, the Devil is powerless; he quickly lets go of God's people and loses the "legal" right to hold on to them. Unforgiveness gives the Devil the legal right to still be there and be in charge, while forgiveness allows God to take full charge and do what He does best—heal, mend the brokenhearted, and set the captives or oppressed free. This is why when we forgive those who have offended us, they become free from the prison of unforgiveness and the enemy's power and influence automatically wither. The Bible says that when we forgive the sins of any, they are forgiven indeed; if we do not forgive them, they are not forgiven (John 20:23).

It is important to understand and always remember that at the very core of the gospel of the kingdom of God is the undisputed truth that salvation comes because of God's grace and is received by placing our faith in Jesus Christ for the forgiveness of our sins. Throughout His ministry here on earth, Jesus used the weapon of forgiveness to recover, restore, and reconcile people to God. Through forgiveness Jesus was able to heal the physical body, as well as the spiritual body. Here are several examples of Jesus using the power of forgiveness during His ministry on earth to set the captives free.

- The paralyzed man lowered on a mat through the roof (Matthew 9:2–8).
- The woman caught in adultery (John 8:3–11).
- The woman who anointed His feet with perfume (Luke 7:44–50).
- Peter, who had denied he knew Jesus (John 18:15–18, 25–27; 21:15–19).
- The criminal on the cross (Luke 23:39–43).
- The people who crucified Him (Luke 23:34).

Forgiveness Is a Key to Your Prayers Being Answered

In the Word of God, we see Jesus not only demonstrating the weapon of forgiveness in action, either to heal or to set the oppressed free, but also frequently teaching His disciples about forgiveness and why they should forgive others. Here are some scriptures that show us Jesus effectively teaching His disciples about the importance of forgiveness.

- "For if you forgive others for their transgressions, your heavenly Father will also forgive you. But if you do not forgive others, then your Father will not forgive your transgressions" (Matthew 6:14–15 NASB).
- "Whenever you stand praying, forgive, if you have anything against anyone, so that your Father who is in heaven will also forgive you your transgressions" (Mark 11:25 NASB).
- "When you pray, say . . . Forgive us our sins, for we ourselves forgive everyone who is indebted to us. And lead us not into temptation" (Luke 11:4 ESV).
- "He said to His disciples, 'It is inevitable that stumbling blocks come, but woe to him through whom they come! It would be better for him if a millstone were hung around his neck and he were thrown into the sea, than that he would cause one of these little ones to stumble. Be on your guard! If your brother sins, rebuke him; and if he repents, forgive him. And if he sins against you seven times a day, and returns to you seven times, saying, "I repent," forgive him'" (Luke 17:1–4 NASB).

- "Then Peter came and said to Him, 'Lord, how often shall my brother sin against me and I forgive him? Up to seven times?' Jesus said to him, 'I do not say to you, up to seven times, but up to seventy times seven'" (Matthew 18:21–22 NASB).

In what is known to us as the Lord's Prayer, Jesus highlighted the principle of forgiving others and being forgiven by God as an attribute of the kingdom of God. Here is Jesus' simple and yet rich and powerful model of fervent prayer:

"Our Father in heaven, Your name be honored as holy. Your kingdom come.
Your will be done on earth as it is in heaven. Give us today our daily bread. And forgive us our debts, as we also have forgiven our debtors. And do not bring us into temptation, but deliver us from the evil one. For Yours is the kingdom and the power and the glory forever. Amen." (Matthew 6:9–13)

Why would Jesus, the master of prayer, include forgiveness in the model prayer? This is a great question and an important one if we are to understand the significance of forgiveness in our spiritual lives. Notice that He says, "Forgive us our debts, as we also *have* forgiven our debtors." This indicates that our prayer or request for forgiveness from God is to come *after* we have first expressed forgiveness to our debtors. By forgiving others we position ourselves to receive forgiveness from God and all the blessings that come from His rule and reign. Furthermore, forgiving others is important because it brings us closer to the presence of God since it illustrates humility, gratitude, and honor before the holy name of God. In other words, forgiveness acts like a key to the doorway of God's presence and power. Jesus emphasized the importance of forgiving others because without a forgiving spirit it is impossible both to be forgiven by God and to walk in the power of His kingdom.

If you want God to hear your prayers and answer them, forgive those who have wronged you and those toward whom you still harbor bitterness and hatred. For the rule and reign of God to move freely in your life and for His will and purpose for your life to be accomplished, you must forgive and continually walk in forgiveness. To do otherwise is to allow the Evil One to lead you into temptation. Forgiveness is your weapon to wage war against the enemy and his kingdom and to create the atmosphere for God's miracles to take place in your life. Before Jesus healed or restored sinners, He forgave them. The outcome was amazing, much to the surprise of the religious people and leaders of His day. In fact, the religious leaders of Jesus' day were extremely upset when Jesus exercised His kingdom authority to forgive sinners (Matthew 9:2–6). Why? Because forgiveness was such a powerful and precious commodity that only God Himself, not mere man, could offer it.

Jesus was and is God in the flesh, so He had, and has, the power to forgive, to heal, and to restore people to God. Today, as disciples of Christ, we have been given the same power, authority, and anointing to forgive and to heal or free those who are still in captivity. Satan wants to discourage God's people from forgiving so that he can neutralize their kingdom authority and power, control and manipulate them, and keep them in the chains of his evil influence. God is ready to hear and answer our prayers if we follow the principles that govern His kingdom, particularly the principle of forgiveness. It is crucial we understand that unforgiveness deeply hinders everything God would like to do through us and hampers our ability to truly represent God as His anointed ambassadors. This is because if we cannot forgive others, then God is not resident in us. Forgiveness is our key to answered prayers, to fighting and winning spiritual battles, and to walking in peace and love.

Fighting a Spiritual Battle

First and foremost, it is important to clearly understand that God, through His Son, Jesus Christ, has already fought and won the battle against Satan on our behalf and rescued us from the power of sin and death. So, why do we have to wage war against Satan and his agents if Jesus has already won the battle for us? The reason is that on a daily basis, Satan sets up traps for God's people, designed to make us stumble into sin. He constantly seeks to corrupt God's spirit in us through offense, false accusation, or opposition. His goal is to destroy the work of God in us and stop us from being channels through whom God's kingdom can be advanced to the ends of the earth. Moreover, Satan attempts to destroy our testimonies, families, and marriages and to destabilize the church and the fellowship of believers in Christ. Thus, it is imperative that we be on guard and ready to fight a spiritual battle through the power of Jesus Christ and from a position of authority and victory. However, there are some fundamentals we need to seriously grasp if are to effectively wage war against the enemy and rescue many from his kingdom.

As we ministered in Africa at a crusade, we were not seeing the power of God move or do mighty things in our midst as we had anticipated. In one particular meeting, demons started manifesting themselves in a young woman, and most of the prayer team went to pray for her. They prayed for her for a long time, but the demons were not completely cast out of her. I also went and prayed for her, but nothing happened. After the meeting we went back to our hotel, and I asked the Lord why we could not cast those demons out of that girl. The Lord began to speak to me and reveal the fundamentals, or essentials, that are required to successfully fight a spiritual battle from a position of authority and victory. Those essentials have changed forever my mentality and the way I go into any spiritual battle. I don't casually go after the kingdom of darkness, and I don't minister without first getting hold of the presence of God and making sure there is nothing in me that may hinder the power of God from moving through me and bringing healing or restoration to those in need.

It is easy to become so familiar with the presence of God or the ways of God that you can be tempted to minister without any consciousness of His presence and holiness. And this is especially true if you have been a minister for a long time and God has used you to do mighty things in other people's lives. In Exodus 33:15, Moses refused to lead God's people or to go forth as God had commanded him unless God's personal presence accompanied them. Moses understood that going anywhere or entering into a battle without God is one of the most dangerous and unwise things a person could ever do. In Mark 3:27 Jesus said, "No one can enter a strong man's house and rob his possession unless he first ties up the strong man. Then he will rob his house." There are things that can tie up the strong man (Satan) and make him powerless. We need to discover exactly what those things are if we are to successfully rescue people from the kingdom of darkness. Just because you are a born-again Christian does not mean you can cast out demons just like that. If you could ask Jesus' disciples, they would tell you. They had walked with and touched the Messiah, but that alone did not mean they had the power to cast out demons (Matthew 17:19). They needed to learn from their Master the principles, or the weapons needed, to plunder the kingdom of darkness. In their case, they needed the weapon of unshakable faith.

Here are three principles I have learned from the Lord that must be in place before we enter into any spiritual battle in our life or on behalf of other people:

- **Do not grieve the Holy Spirit.** The first principle God revealed to me was to never grieve the Holy Spirit because He is the one who activates the power of God. How do we grieve the Holy Spirit, or bring sorrow to Him? We do it through bitterness, anger, harsh words, and slander (Ephesians 4:30–31).
- **Refrain from anger.** Anger leads to defeat. It gives Satan a case against us and empowers him to resist our attempts to drive him away (Psalm 37:8).
- **Forgive and Repent.** As we forgive those who have offended us, God opens the floodgates of heaven so that miracle after miracle begins to pour down. Repentance (turning away from sin) also is important because it lifts off us every hindrance in our lives.

It is almost impossible for a person seeking deliverance to be delivered without repentance or while holding onto bitterness, anger, and resentment. Forgiveness is a divine power that sets things in motion.

The day after the Lord revealed these simple principles to me, the young woman who had been tormented by demons again showed up, this time at our last service on a Sunday. I said, "Thank You, Lord!" When it was time for prayers, I went over to the girl and asked her to repent of her sins and let go of the bitterness the Lord said was in her heart. When she did so, she cried loudly, and we commanded the demons to loose her, and she was loosed. God moved unrestricted in the girl's life because she had released everything that belonged to the enemy. Unforgiveness, bitterness, hatred, and anger belong to the enemy. Let go of your bitterness, and you will experience freedom.

Never fight your spiritual battle in anger or bitterness; that is fighting from a position of defeat. It will leave you defeated and knocked out by the enemy before you even step into the ring with him. Fight with the joy of the Lord, in faith, and without any resentment by forgiving all your enemies. In so doing, you will be fighting from a victorious position. Before you pray, forgive; before you praise, forgive; and before you worship, forgive. Do this, and you shall see the power of God manifested in your life like nothing you have ever seen before. Without forgiveness and repentance, it is difficult for the Holy Spirit to move. Forgiveness and repentance invites and welcomes the Holy Spirit and allows Him to work on our behalf. The Holy Spirit cannot impose Himself on us if we don't want Him. Forgiveness invites Him in and shuts the door to the enemy.

If we, the people of God and the body of Christ, can learn to rid our hearts of offense, bitterness, and resentment, we are going to see the mighty powers of God move in our midst and in the nations of the world. Spiritual fathers and mothers need to forgive their sons and daughters, and sons and daughters need to forgive their spiritual fathers and mothers, if we are to welcome and activate the power of the Holy Spirit in us. God-fearing men and women need to rise up in the power of the Spirit and of the living and mighty God and wage warfare against the spirit of disunity that is engulfing the body of Christ through offense. Our battle is not against flesh and blood but against the rulers, powers, and forces of darkness (Ephesians 6:12). Thank God "the weapons of our warfare are not worldly, but are powerful through God for the demolition of strongholds" (2 Corinthians 10:4).

When you are offended in any way, do not go after the people who have offended you. Instead, go after the kingdom of darkness, and use the weapon of forgiveness and prayer to defeat the purposes of the enemy. Forgiveness is a mighty weapon of God that pulls down every stronghold.

God has given us powerful weapons of spiritual warfare to use daily against the schemes of Satan. It is unfortunate that many people do not know yet how to use the spiritual weapons of God and wage successful spiritual warfare against Satan's attacks. Consequently, many Christians end up defeated, disappointed, and bogged down to the point of questioning God's ability and power to deliver them from Satan's attacks. God has given us power and authority over Satan, but most of us don't know how to use that power. One of the reasons we fail to use our weapons of spiritual warfare effectively to win the battles against Satan is because we fight from a position of bitterness, hatred, anger, pride, and unforgiveness and not from a position of humility. As we have already stated, offense that is not dealt with leads to sin, and where there is sin, there is defeat.

Four Powerful Spiritual Weapons

To wage successful spiritual warfare against the forces of darkness, you need to use the weapons God has made available to you, and you must fight, not in anger or with a bitter heart, but with the spirit of love. Fighting in anger and bitterness can cost you your victory. Too many people are spiritually defeated because they try to fight their spiritual battles with anger, bitterness, resentment, and unforgiveness still in their hearts. Your first step in the spiritual battle is forgiveness. Then move on to read the Word of God. After you have read the Word of God, enter into praise and worship, and then make your requests known to God through prayer. If you begin with prayer or with praise and worship without letting go of your offenses, your breakthrough will be hindered. Here are four powerful weapons of our warfare, given in the order they are to be used:

- **The weapon of forgiveness**: Repent; forgive or ask for forgiveness.
- **The weapon of the Word of God**: Read the Word of God for empowerment and strength to speak God's Word into your life situation.
- **The weapon of praise and worship**: Glorify, praise, worship, and uplift the victorious name of God, and thus generate an atmosphere for the Holy Spirit to move and open the heavens.

- **The weapon of prayer:** Finally, ask God for whatever you need from Him, and wait upon Him to give you direction.

It is important to understand that God is a God of order and He works in an orderly way. Forgiveness should be the first weapon we use, even before we use the Word of God, praise and worship, and prayer. Forgiveness is what breaks down resistance, stubbornness, and any strongholds in the spiritual realm. Each time I have forgiven or a person to whom I am ministering has forgiven, God has moved in a very powerful way. We can't win the battle against the Devil when we are full of anger, bitterness, unforgiveness, and hatred. We first must tie him down through forgiveness, the Word of God, and God's love.

The subject of forgiveness is paramount to the body of Christ and to every Christian who has a desire and a heart to advance the kingdom of God. Forgiveness is much needed in the body of Christ because the enemy has poured out the spirit of anger and hatred upon the earth, causing divisions in the church, in the nations, in marriages, and in people's relationships. As the body of Christ, we can't function in the world today and unleash the kingdom of God or God's government here on earth without the spirit of forgiveness and love.

Forgiveness is not a feeling, just as love is not a feeling. It is a choice, and those who make the choice to walk in forgiveness and love are capable of forcefully advancing the kingdom of God. Kingdom people are called to forgive the sins of sinners, not once, not twice, and not even thrice, but with no limits because God's forgiveness, mercy, and love have no limits. Satan cannot withstand the weapon of forgiveness because he loses his grip on the forgiven. And when God forgives our sins, we become His possession and His people, marked by His love and Christ's righteousness.

Finally, we need to remember that because we belong to God and we are anointed to do the work and business of His kingdom, the world will reject, persecute, and offend us. We should never take this personally, however, because we are a people *in* this world but not *of* this world. Rejection or offense is not the end of the world; in fact, it gives us an opportunity to demonstrate the love, mercy, and forgiving heart of God.

Jesus was rejected, abused, beaten, and crucified, but in the end He used the weapon of forgiveness to forgive the very people who rejected and killed Him. Forgiveness is one of the most powerful weapons you can use to win spiritual battles in your life. With it you can beat diseases, depression, and stress and bring down every stronghold. Use it, and you will never be defeated, shaken, or moved in life. Your joy, happiness, confidence, and purpose will be restored, and God's vision in your life will be illuminated. Each time you forgive, God steps into your heart and Satan steps out; and when God is in you and with you, nothing is impossible.

A Prayer for Deliverance from Unforgiveness

Father, I surrender all my bitterness, hatred, anger, and resentment I have toward _____. I forgive them and release them out of my heart in the power of the name that is above every name, the name of Jesus Christ. In Jesus' name I forgive everyone who has wronged me, offended me, or taken advantage of me. I totally surrender my heart to the power of the Holy Spirit to bring healing to my hurting soul, to transform me, and to help me walk in the love and mercy of God in Jesus' name. I therefore unleash the weapon of forgiveness upon the enemy's camp and release every person held in captivity by the enemy because of my anger and bitterness, and in Jesus' name I release myself from the influence and power of the unforgiving spirit. Today I declare that I will walk and live above offense and in the love of God, no matter what the situation or circumstance may be. May You alone, God, be my defender, protector, and shelter, and may the blood of Jesus Christ cover me 24/7 in Jesus' name. No weapon or tactic of the enemy shall prosper against me from now on and forevermore. My God, You will go before me and lead me as I put my trust in Your power and ability to do extraordinary things in my life. Amen!

Chapter 8

WHY FORGIVE?

IN THE PREVIOUS CHAPTER, WE FOCUSED ON FORGIVENESS AS A WEAPON OF GOD AND noted that when we forgive, Satan no longer has a hold on us or on those we have forgiven. Satan loses his grip and authority over people when we forgive them, and God through the power of the Holy Spirit takes full charge over them.

Throughout the previous chapters of this book, we have stated a number of reasons why we should forgive those who willingly and knowingly—or unknowingly—offend us. In this chapter we will dig deeper to learn more about why we should forgive and walk in forgiveness.

Advancing God's Kingdom

To those reasons stated previously, we can add that advancing God's kingdom is another very important reason why we should forgive. If we would like God to use us mightily in these difficult and challenging times, we need to discover and reflect God's grace, mercy, love, and forgiving heart to a world burning with hatred and anger.

Nowadays people everywhere seem to be angry and upset. They are angry with God, with the government, with their families or friends, with a certain people group, or with the church and its leadership. Everywhere we look, we see offended and angry people. Small, insignificant issues easily spark deadly fires of dispute, division, divorce, and hatred. I believe very strongly that the church is the vehicle of God's unity, peace, and stability to this unstable world. However, we, the church, need to get hold of the heart of God and let His character and nature consume us so that we can be that vehicle that brings peace, unity, stability, healing, and life to this hurting world. One thing is certain: We cannot be a vehicle of God that brings restoration to this broken world if we too are living or behaving just like the world—full of bitterness, anger, and hatred. We must first allow God's fire to burn out of us the spirit of hatred, bitterness, anger, and unforgiveness. Hatred and anger not only stop us from demonstrating the power of God here on earth but also stop us from inspiring lost souls to turn to God and to His kingdom. If the world sees that we are just as they are—unforgiving, hurtful, bitter, and angry—they will not desire the God we claim to have, because we are no different from them.

Do you want to advance the kingdom of God? Do you want to let God work through you to change the world? Do you want to be a symbol of the presence and power of God? Do you want to demonstrate His character and nature to this lost world? Do you want to be a symbol of peace, unity, and God's salvation in your family and in your community? If your answer to these questions is yes, then you need to understand how you can effectively be God's vehicle of transformation, reformation, and revival in society. Activating the nature of God's heart in you is the key to winning the lost and motivating others to serve God. You can have the best message in town, the fire of God, the presence of God, and the living water bubbling inside of you, but if you don't have the gracious heart of God and are full of hatred, nobody will run to you to seek what you have. Hatred, anger, and bad attitudes bring corruption to everything good God has placed in your care, and they keep you from rescuing people from the hands of the enemy.

Proverbs 22:1 clearly tells us, "A good reputation is more desirable than great wealth, and favorable acceptance more than silver and gold" (ISV). As Christ's ambassadors, it is extremely important to understand that if the things of this world corrupt our reputation (or "name," as other versions translate it), we can never make an impact for God in society. We can have the presence and power of God in us, but people will not run to us for help because we, the containers, have been corrupted.

This is what the spirit of unforgiveness, or walking with the spirit of bitterness, hatred, and anger, does to the vessels of God. In order for us to win the lost and offended for the kingdom of God and be the source of God's life, we need to allow God to change us from the inside out so that everything about us and in us reflects the glory of His holy name.

If we are unforgiving, arrogant, and ungracious in our speech, we might pray, fast, and intercede, but we are not likely to see one soul saved because our character is a hindrance to the lost. God has not called us to live our Christian lives on Sundays only and only within the four walls of our assembly. Rather, we are to demonstrate His love and character every day of our lives and outside the four walls of the church—in our speech, conduct, attitude, and character. We attract people to God and are recognized in the world as true children or disciples of Jesus Christ when we walk in humility, mercy, love, and forgiveness. When I gave my life to the Lord, the Lord clearly said to me, "Change your outward attitude and character, and people will desire the inner substance I have placed in you." Since then, God has used me to win souls for His kingdom and to inspire people to follow Him because I clothe myself with His name and reputation wherever I go and I desire to represent His kingdom, even if it means losing my dignity or looking like a fool.

When we walk in forgiveness, love, and mercy and show grace to others, we clothe ourselves with God's reputation, or name. People then begin to see God in us and through us. They see His majestic glory, love, and mercy, and they begin to desire Him and thirst for His presence in their lives.

So why should we forgive? We should forgive immediately when we are offended, either by a fellow Christian or a worldly person, so that we can demonstrate the true character of God's gracious and forgiving heart. Many of us have failed to witness to those we know and those who know us well because we may have said or done something for which we never apologized, or they may have done something to us and we responded in bitterness and never forgave them. As a result, they question our Christianity or even the God we serve. Forgiving others or asking for forgiveness breaks down the barriers and answers people's doubts about God. Our humility and a changed attitude inspire people to follow God.

We should forgive people and ask people to forgive us so that we can restore God's reputation in our lives. We must desire to be deeply immersed in God's forgiving nature so that wherever we go, we can declare freedom to the captives and announce the arrival of the rule and reign of God's kingdom in the hearts of people. Forgiveness is a powerful and extremely important tool of evangelism. Remember, your lifestyle is an important part of evangelism and everything you claim to be in God. You can't claim to be influenced by God while acting otherwise. Unforgiveness blinds people from seeing God's glory, love, and mercy in you. Remember, before people experience the presence of God and meet Him, they will meet you and experience Him through your character, speech, and everything in you. So give no room to offense, slander, gossip, or bitterness in your life. You are the light of God.

The Cost of Anger and Bitterness Is Your Destiny

Another important reason we should forgive is that anger and bitterness can stop us from stepping into our destiny in life or from seeing the fulfillment of God's promises in our lives. Furthermore, it can stop us from doing the work of God with fear and trembling in the light of His holiness. To God, the spirit or motive behind what we do for His kingdom is more important than what we actually do for Him. We can do the right things for Him and yet do them with a wrong motive or attitude or with a bitter heart. It is our attitude toward what we do for Him that brings the greatest honor and glory to His holy name.

In Numbers 20 we find a very good example of the cost of doing the right thing for God but with a bitter and angry heart or attitude. In Exodus 17:6, God commanded the great Moses to strike a rock. God promised Moses He would make water flow out of the rock to satisfy the thirsty people. Moses obeyed and did exactly what the Lord commanded him to do—he struck the rock, and water came out of it. Moses did this with a proper attitude. In Numbers 20, however, we see a different scenario. The Israelites, as was their custom during the wilderness journey, complained again against Moses and Aaron over their lack of water. They said to them, "Why have you brought the LORD's assembly into this wilderness for us and our livestock to die here? Why have you led us up from Egypt to bring us to this evil place? It's not a place of grain, figs, vines, and pomegranates, and there is no water to drink!" (verses 4–5).

Moses and Aaron went into the presence of God. They fell down with their faces to the ground, and the glory of the Lord appeared to them. Then the Lord spoke to Moses with specific instructions.

> *"Take the staff and assemble the community. You and your brother Aaron are to speak to the rock [not strike it] while they watch, and it will yield its water. You will bring out water for them from the rock and provide drink for the community and their livestock." So Moses took the staff from the LORD's presence just as He had commanded him. Moses and Aaron summoned the assembly in front of the rock, and Moses said to them, "Listen, you rebels! Must we bring water out of this rock for you?" Then Moses raised his hand and struck the rock twice [showing his annoyance and frustration] with his staff, so that a great amount of water gushed out, and the community and their livestock drank."* (Numbers 20:8–11)

By striking the rock twice instead of speaking to it, and by calling the assembly of God "rebels," Moses clearly indicated he was upset and extremely angry at the people.

Moses had had enough of the people's complaints and unappreciative hearts toward Yahweh, who had miraculously delivered them from the hands of the wicked Pharaoh through the miracle of the plagues (Exodus 7–11) and the crossing of the Red Sea (14:15–27). In the wilderness, the Lord had faithfully—and miraculously—provided water (17:1–6) and food (16:13–15). Moses had the right to be angry and upset about the people's attitude, but he let his anger consume his heart and influence his actions. He responded to the people's grumbling without any regard for the reputation of God. God knew the people of Israel of that day were a rebellious bunch, but as the leader over them, Moses was not to take the people's complaints or insults personally but rather take them to the

Lord, who had called him to lead the people. The people's complaints against Moses and Aaron constituted rebellion against God Himself, so it was up to God to deal with them.

Moses was to be a shepherd and a steward of God's people. He was in charge of leading them as God commanded him to; all other matters were to be left in the hands of God almighty. Moses' response to the people's complaints should have been to look to God, as he had done all along, and intercede for them to have a changed heart. But again this was not the first time Moses showed his anger at the people. In Exodus 32:19, when Moses came down from the mountain and found the people dancing and worshiping a golden calf Aaron had made for them, Moses became enraged—and rightly so. But he let his anger get the best of him, and he smashed the two tablets on which God had inscribed His instructions for the people. In that case, God did not get angry at Moses, maybe because Moses acted out of a holy anger at the people for replacing the worship of the only living and true God with the worship of a golden calf. But in the case of striking the rock instead of speaking to it as God instructed him, Moses was acting out of his personal feelings of anger and not out of a holy anger.

Holy anger is that which is properly directed toward the promotion of ungodliness in the society or the teaching of false doctrines. In Matthew 21:12–13 Jesus exhibited a holy anger against the money changers who had turned the house of the Lord into a marketplace. He knocked over the tables of the money changers and the chairs of those selling doves because zeal for the Lord and for the house of the Lord consumed Him.

Judging by God's response to Moses' striking the rock instead of speaking to it, we can safely say that Moses' anger this time around was not a holy anger. Consequently, God punished him and said to him and Aaron, "Because you did not trust Me to show My holiness in the sight of the Israelites, you will not bring this assembly into the land I have given them" (Numbers 20:12). One act of anger cost Moses entrance into the Promised Land, even after all his hard work and dedication. Think about that for a second! Anger can lead you to act in an ungodly way and can cost you the promises of God upon your life and your future. How many people are sitting in prisons around the world today because of one act of anger? How many people have forfeited their positions or jobs in the corporate world because of one act of anger? And how many souls have left the body of Christ or leave churches simply because of one act of anger? The numbers are countless. God wants to restore the church, the body of Christ, first through forgiveness and reconciliation and then through reformation and revival. There can never be true revival without reconciliation and forgiveness among the body of Christ. Forgiveness is key to igniting a revival fire in the nations and to peace and stability both in the body of Christ and in the nations of the world.

One big lesson we learn from the account of Moses is that God takes His word and instructions very seriously, regardless of what people may have done or not done. As ministers of the gospel, we are to preach in love, rebuke in love, and share God's Word from a forgiving and gracious heart and not from a hurtful or bitter heart. As ministers of the gospel and disciples of Jesus Christ, we are to walk in forgiveness at all times so that we can share the Word of God with a pure, humble, and gracious heart. Yes, people are sinners and extremely difficult, and God knows that—and we know that too. But as shepherds and stewards of God's people and as disciples of Jesus Christ, we must lead and share the gospel with extreme patience, extravagant love, and complete obedience to God's instructions.

Never take matters into your own hands or take opposition or offense personally. When you do that, you risk losing your patience, your Christlike love for people, and your temper. Ungodly anger is dangerous because it destroys your future and destiny and it pollutes your reputation. Remember, God will hold you accountable for what you do and how you do what He has called you to do for His kingdom. If the great Moses, who saw God face to face, was held accountable for disregarding God's instructions because of his anger, how much more will God hold us accountable for disobeying Him out of our anger? Fear God, and do His work and will in humility and not in anger or resentment, regardless of offense or how hurt your feelings might be. As a stable and mature Christian, you are to demonstrate extraordinary love, patience, and humility for the sake of the name of the Lord. Show your godly love to the unlovable and to those who are inconsistent in their character so that, through you, they may come to know and to experience the true love and mercy of God.

Forgiveness Proves Our Love and Connection to God

Another important reason why we should forgive others is that forgiveness really proves or demonstrates that we love God, that we are true sons and daughters of God who are deeply connected to Him as true disciples. In John 13:34–35 Jesus said to His disciples, "I give you a new command: Love one another. Just as I have loved you, you must also love one another. By this all people will know that you are My disciples, if you have love for one another." God's love for us and our love for Him and for other believers is a distinguishing mark of Jesus' disciples and kingdom people. In Matthew 5:43-48 Jesus also taught His disciples to extend their love even to their enemies. This is because love is God's powerful weapon that reveals His true nature and character to the world. It is also crucial to understand that God's love is not a feeling but a choice. We choose to love people who don't "measure up" to Him so that through His love they can be connected to Him through Christ, the only Person who does measure up to the righteousness of God. So when we talk of God's love, we are not talking about the "feelings of love"; we are talking about God's unconditional choice to love people—that is, to seek what is best for them—regardless of their sinful nature. It is this unconditional choice to love those who do not deserve to be loved but instead deserve to be punished that demonstrates the gravity of God's forgiveness and love.

We are to emulate God's extraordinary love so that we can choose to forgive people even before they ask us for forgiveness. We can do this because neither love nor forgiveness is a feeling but a choice. If you are waiting to *feel* love for a person or to *feel* forgiveness inside of you before you forgive, you will never effectively forgive. Forgiveness and love are free gifts that must be given to the underserved person. Just as God made a choice to forgive our sins, we must make a choice to forgive those who have wronged us. The apostle Paul wrote to the church at Colossae:

> *Holy and loved, put on heartfelt compassion, kindness, humility, gentleness, and patience, accepting one another and forgiving one another if anyone has a complaint against another. Just as the Lord has forgiven you, so you must also forgive. Above all, put on love—the perfect bond of unity. And let the peace of the Messiah, to which you were also called in one body, control your hearts. Be thankful.* (Colossians 3:12–15)

In the verses just prior to this (Colossians 3:5–8), Paul had commanded the believers to put away worldly behaviors such as anger, wrath, malice, slander, and filthy language. Then he moved on to command them to put on compassion, kindness, humility, gentleness, and patience. Why? Because without heartfelt compassion, kindness, humility, gentleness, and patience, no human being can choose to walk in love and forgiveness. The truth is that a person cannot truly love another person without having a heartfelt compassion or humility that flows from the compassionate heart of God. Forgiveness and love define our relationship with God and with other people, and they prove the depth of our connection to the forgiving kingdom of God. In 1 John 4:20, John says, "If anyone says, 'I love God,' yet hates his brother, he is a liar. For the person who does not love his brother he has seen cannot love the God he has not seen." He further states in 1 John 3:14, "We know that we have passed from death to life, because we love each other. Anyone who does not love remains in death" (NIV). Love is the exact opposite of unforgiveness, envy, jealousy, hate, pride, and bitterness. You cannot truly love somebody and hold bitterness or unforgiveness against him or her at the same time.

The Forgiving Heart of God Illustrated

In Matthew 18:23–35 Jesus illustrated through the parable of the unforgiving servant the compassionate and forgiving heart of God that is to be our model. In the parable, the servant owed the king ten thousand talents, which he could not repay when the time to settle the debt with the king arrived. The king commanded that the man's wife, children, and everything he had be sold to pay the debt. However, the servant asked the king to have patience with him, and because the king had a compassionate heart, he released the servant and forgave his debt as if it never even existed. The king's choice to forgive the debt of his servant illustrates God's forgiving heart. In the parable, the king is a symbol of God, who because of His compassionate heart, chose to forgive our enormous debt of sin. But watch what the forgiven servant did to his fellow servant who owed him only one hundred denarii. He mercilessly grabbed him, choked him, and demanded the money he was owed. Why would the forgiven man respond like that? It could only be because he had no gratitude or compassion in his heart. A person who is thankful for the kind gift of forgiveness he or she has received from God can easily extend forgiveness to others. The ungrateful have no compassion and love for other people. They are glad to receive forgiveness, but they do not want to give it.

In the parable of the two lost sons (better known as the parable of the prodigal son) in Luke 15:11–32, Jesus again illustrated the forgiving heart of God. The younger son had asked for his inheritance from his father while his father was still alive. His father gave him his share, and "he set off for a distant country and there squandered his wealth in wild living. After he had spent everything, there was a severe famine in that whole country, and he began to be in need" (verses 13–14 NIV). He looked for a job and was hired to work in a field feeding pigs. He was starving to the point that he longed to fill his stomach with what the pigs were eating, but no one gave him anything.

> *"When he came to his senses, he said, 'How many of my father's hired servants have food to spare, and here I am starving to death! I will set out and go back to my father and say to him: Father, I have sinned against heaven and against you. I am no longer worthy to be called your son; make me like one of your hired servants.' So he got up and went to his father. But while he was still a long way off, his father saw him and was filled with compassion for him; he ran to his son, threw his arms around him and kissed him."* (Luke 15:17–20 NIV)

As we can tell in the account, the father did not ask any questions or say, "I warned you" or "I told you so." Because of his compassion, he was moved to run to his son, throw his arms around him, and kiss him. The father could have chosen to punish or ignore his lost but returning son, but because he was compelled by unconditional love, he chose to forgive. The older brother chose to be angry with both his father and his younger brother, because he was self-centered and had no compassion in his heart whatsoever (Luke 15:25–30). The father in the parable is a symbol of God the Father, while the elder brother can be compared to those who are still in the house of the Lord but full of self-righteousness and with no compassion for the lost. God's forgiveness always flows from His compassionate heart. He does not forgive us based on what we have done for Him.

Forgiveness clearly is one of the greatest gifts God has ever given to us. Our sins have been forgiven, not because of our righteousness, but because of His righteousness. So what does this mean to us? This means that just as we have freely received the gift of forgiveness from God, we are to give the gift of forgiveness freely to other people.

If you refuse to forgive, then you are saying that you are righteous and you have never sinned or offended anybody. Let God's compassion, love, mercy, and gracious heart be your heart. You are born for such a time as this to demonstrate the warmth, tenderness, mercy, and love of God. Be what God has called you to be, and God will be what He has promised to be to you. If you are merciful, kind, tenderhearted, and caring toward others, God will be merciful, kind, tenderhearted, and caring toward you and your household.

In a nutshell, we should forgive because:

- Unforgiveness shows we do not really love Jesus (John 15:12).
- Unforgiveness stops God from forgiving our sins (Matthew 6:15).
- Unforgiveness opens us up to terrible consequences (Matthew 18:23–35).
- Unforgiveness can hinder God from answering our prayers (Mark 11:24–25).
- Unforgiveness can defile a person spiritually (Hebrews 12:15).

- Unforgiveness can give Satan an advantage over us (2 Corinthians 2:10–11).
- Unforgiveness can keep a person out of the kingdom of God (Matthew 7:12, 21).

Many people today are suffering or failing to succeed in life because of the curses unforgiveness has brought upon them. And many more people suffer mental and emotional problems, physical problems, financial problems, divorce, or can't grow spiritually from one level to another because of unforgiveness. Simply through the power of forgiveness, you can change the course of your life and receive fresh anointing, direction, and blessings from God. When the power of forgiveness is released, it destroys every stronghold in your life and sets a path for the power of God to move in your life like never before. Forgiveness brings inner healing, restores your confidence, and clears away all your shame.

Let God uproot any unforgiving spirit in you and cleanse your heart from every past hurt and pain. Declare freedom to everybody who has offended you and forgiveness from anybody you may have offended. Don't feel ashamed. This is very important. In fact, your life depends on it, and their life depends on it. In our next chapter, we will touch on the importance of repentance or asking for forgiveness. Asking for forgiveness or repenting of our shortcomings is extremely important. In fact, effective forgiveness cannot take place without repentance.

The Benefits of Forgiving Others

In concluding this chapter, let us consider some of the benefits of walking in the spirit of forgiveness and forgiving others:

- **God will avenge you:** "Friends, do not avenge yourselves; instead, leave room for His wrath. For it is written: Vengeance belongs to Me; I will repay, says the Lord" (Romans 12:19; cf. Leviticus 19:18; Deuteronomy 32:35; Psalm 94:1; Proverbs 20:22; 24:29; Romans 12:17).

- **You will not give the Devil an opportunity to influence your life through anger:** "Be angry and do not sin. Don't let the sun go down on your anger, and don't give the Devil an opportunity" (Ephesians 4:26–27).
- **You will be happy, loving, merciful, and both physically and spiritually healthier because you don't have any grudges in your life to weigh you down:** "Do not take revenge or bear a grudge against members of your community, but love your neighbor as yourself; I am Yahweh" (Leviticus 19:18; cf. Matthew 5:44; 1 Peter 3:9; Proverbs 24:17–19, 29).
- **God will forgive your wrongdoing and answer your prayers:** "And whenever you stand praying, if you have anything against anyone, forgive him, so that your Father in heaven will also forgive you your wrongdoing" (Mark 11:25; cf. Matthew 5:23–24; Luke 6:37).
- **You will conquer the enemy with God's goodness and overpower him:** "Do not be conquered by evil, but conquer evil with good" (Romans 12:21).

When you forgive people, you are identifying yourself with God and His kingdom and you will never allow the things of this world to distract you and lead you away from the presence of God. Because of a forgiving heart, you will not be shaken by any offense or persecution, just as Jesus was unshaken during His trials.

Chapter 9

EFFECTUAL FORGIVENESS

WE CAN ALL TESTIFY (UNLESS WE ARE FROM ANOTHER PLANET) THAT FORGIVING SOMEONE who has wronged us can be one of the most difficult things in life to do. It is especially difficult for a person who has never known or experienced forgiveness from God and has no fear of Him and true love for Him. It is fearing and loving God, as well as loving other people, that helps us to forgive people, and this is at the heart of the two most important commandments: Love your God with all your heart, and love your neighbor as yourself (Matthew 22:34-40). Reverence and honor for God is key to a consistent lifestyle of living under the power of God's own nature and bringing glory to His holy name by maintaining a right attitude toward God and toward people. Because we fear God and want to maintain our fellowship with Him and walk in peace with others, we will forgive and not seek revenge, even when we have a great opportunity to make our offender pay for what he or she has done against us.

Forgiveness, Fear, and Humility

David is a great example of what it means to fear God. His life demonstrates how the fear of God and our loyalty to Him can stop us from seeking vengeance, even when it is within our power to do so. Saul the king was jealous of David and hated him. This was not because David had done anything wrong against Saul, however, but simply because David was a very popular young man as a result of successfully accomplishing everything Saul sent him to do (1 Samuel 18:5). Saul's hatred for David started when David returned from defeating the Philistines. He became furious and resentful when the women came out from all the cities of Israel to meet him, singing and dancing with tambourines, with shouts of joy, proclaiming, "Saul has killed his thousands, but David his tens of thousands" (verse 7).

These praises for David annoyed the king greatly. "Saul was furious and resented this song. 'They credited tens of thousands to David,' he complained, 'but they only credited me with thousands. What more can he have but the kingdom?' So Saul watched David jealously from that day forward" (I Samuel 18:8–9). Saul's anger and jealousy developed into insecurity and hatred. From that moment on, all he desired or wanted was to kill David as soon as he possibly could. As we learn in the biblical account, Saul attempted to kill David on many occasions, but the Lord protected David and shielded him from Saul's evil heart.

Now, what makes this account so important to us is David's response to Saul's hatred and attempts on his life and particularly his reaction after he had a perfect opportunity to kill Saul. In 1 Samuel 24, we see that David easily could have killed Saul when Saul, seeking to relieve himself, entered the cave where David and his men were hiding from the king. In fact, some of David's men told David, "Look, this is the day the Lord told you about: 'I will hand your enemy over to you so you can do to him whatever you desire'" (verse 4). This sounds like good spiritual advice from David's men. After all, if David killed Saul, he could say, "God has finally answered my prayers and delivered my great enemy, Saul, into my hands."

Instead, David secretly cut off the corner of Saul's robe. While David had no intention whatsoever of killing Saul, it seems he wanted to scare him just a little bit. But notice David's reaction after he had secretly cut off the corner of Saul's robe. His conscience bothered him for doing so, and he said to his men, "'I swear before the Lord: I would never do such a thing to my lord, the Lord's anointed. I will never lift my hand against him, since he is the Lord's anointed.' With these words David persuaded his men, and he did not let them rise up against Saul" (verses 6–7). What caused David to refrain from killing Saul when he had the opportunity to do so? And what caused him to regret cutting off even the corner of Saul's robe? By looking at David's reaction after he had cut off the corner of the king's robe, we can safely say that David's reverential fear and honor for God in his heart and His respect for God's anointed leaders stopped him from killing Saul. Those attitudes also caused his inner spirit to be bothered so that he swore never to do that again and persuaded his men not to rise up against Saul. David's conscience guided him to respond in a righteous way by forgiving the king and not counting Saul's attempts on his life against him.

Most people in David's position would have taken that opportunity to kill their enemy, especially when they had the support of their friends saying, "Look, this is the day the Lord told you about: 'I will hand your enemy over to you so you can do to him whatever you desire.'" And many more would have justified their retaliation by saying, "He tried to kill me many times before; this was my opportunity to kill him before he killed me."

How does this account speak to us? It speaks to the atrocities we have committed in the body of Christ against leaders God has placed over us. Through our gossip or slander in retaliation for their shortcomings or mistakes, we have "killed" them. We have not killed them physically, of course, but spiritually by name-calling, questioning their leadership, and degrading their gifts and God's calling over their lives—all because of their actions toward us. We must be careful, just as David was careful, not to touch God's anointed ones, regardless of their shortcomings. Rather, we should respond to their carelessness or mistreatment of us in the fear of God, forgiving them and praying for them. God Himself will deal with their shortcomings, just as He did with Saul.

To forgive effectively, you do not need to count the wrongs done against you and remove all the "whys" and "why nots." In fact, when you begin to count all the wrongs done against you, your mind will begin to consider all the reasons you should seek revenge and not forgive or show mercy to your enemy. David spared Saul's life because he had no offense in his heart and he knew fully well he had done nothing evil against Saul and his leadership. David was just doing what God had anointed him to do as a powerful commander of the army and as the young, up-and-coming leader of Israel. Furthermore, David would not take matters into his own hands and kill Saul because he was a humble young man who put his trust in God. He said to Saul, "May the LORD judge between you and me, and may the LORD take vengeance on you for me, but my hand will never be against you. As the old proverb says, 'Wickedness comes from wicked people.' My hand will never be against you" (1 Samuel 24:12–13). David's humble attitude not only shows us how godly people who fear and love God ought to be, but it also explains why God considered David the apple of His eye.

In order for us to discharge someone from a fault or wrongdoing and not seek revenge, we need humility, as well as respect for God, for those He has placed in leadership, and for each other. David was a man who respected and honored God, and where there is fear of God and honor for His holy name, there is mercy, love, grace, and forgiveness.

It is important to know that some people may be motivated to oppose you, attack you, or bring you down, not because you have done anything wrong against them, but simply because God's hand of blessing is upon you. This is why defending yourself is of little use; people will oppose you no matter what you do. If you start defending yourself or trying to explain yourself, you will never win against them because their hatred toward you is not really about you as a person but about God and His blessings and presence in your life.

Knowing you cannot make everybody happy or make them love you removes from you a "man-pleasing spirit," a performance mentality, and false humility. This is important because this makes it easier to walk in forgiveness and to live in humility and peace, allowing God to be real in your life and to be the center of your soul. When your humility is fake and not centered on bringing glory to God by honoring and respecting people, your spiritual life will be a life of "performance" designed to please man, not God. And above all, it will be very difficult for you to forgive or ask forgiveness. Be real, and let God be the center of your life. That will help you to walk in His love and power and also help you to rise above every criticism and offense. If you are hurt or unhappy with someone or offended by someone, don't hide your feelings because they will build up like a pressure cooker and blow up one day, and the damage will be costly. Deal with every offense, either by seeking forgiveness or by forgiving or by sitting down with the person who may have offended you. Realize that sometimes people may do something with no intention whatsoever of trying to hurt you or bring harm to you. Don't live a life based on assumptions, speculations, or presumption. You will not live a life of regrets if, before you act, you think, pray, and seek the face of God.

Having a deeper understanding of the enemy's tactic of using offense against you to shift your focus away from God and destabilize your spiritual life, marriage, relationships with others, and fellowship with the Holy Spirit will save your life and help you not to take things too personally. The secret to living for God in an ungodly atmosphere and offensive world is to build a strong spiritual foundation in your life and allow the Holy Spirit to rule and reign in your heart. When you have a strong foundation, you can withstand every test and not allow offense to spoil what God wants to do in you and through you. Finally, if you know you have done nothing wrong and yet some people hate you, don't seek to justify yourself; let the glory and the light of God shine in you so that through you they can see God and find His love and mercy. However, if people are unhappy with you because of your ungodly living or unrepentant heart, then you need to make some adjustments in your life and allow the Holy Spirit to transform you.

We are not perfect people because we live in an imperfect world; thus we too can make mistakes. But we must be willing to do something about it and allow God to correct us and restore us.

Emotional Forgiveness

Effectual forgiveness is achieved by forgiving from the depths of your heart and not from your emotions. Forgiving as a mere emotional act is dangerous. Many people who forgive from their emotions have a hard time letting go of an offense because the hurts are still hidden in the core of their being, which is the heart. People who forgive with their emotions only are able to tell you exactly when, what time, which day, and which year so and so offended them. They are able to count how many times they have been offended and they have forgiven—all because they have not released the bitterness of offense from their heart. In fact, they nurture their pain, anger, hatred, and hurt by reminding the person who offended them of it or by sharing with multiple people what that person did against them. Many relationships today are destroyed beyond repair as a result of forgiveness that is merely of the *emotions* and not of the *heart*. Emotional forgiveness is weak and ineffective because it flows from a person's emotions and not from the real him or her—which is the heart. The heart is the reflection of who we really are and what we are all about. When we truly forgive from the depths of our heart, all the hurts are flushed out, and love and mercy begin to flow in our heart like a river of living water.

Many people struggle with unforgiveness simply because they have forgiven their offenders emotionally, and that is not true forgiveness. It is a big mistake because a decision made on the basis of emotions has no influence or conviction in a person's heart. How do you know you have forgiven only emotionally and not from your heart? If you are constantly bringing up past offenses and feeling bitter when the person who offended you is around, then you have not fully forgiven the person or let go of the offense. But when you have peace and love in you and no hateful feelings when you are around the person who offended you, then you have truly forgiven that person and let go of the offense.

The work of the Holy Spirit of God is crucial to forgiving effectively. Not only does He bring healing and restoration into our heart, help us to walk in love, and convict us of sin, but He also empowers us to forgive unconditionally. Forgiving out of our emotions is simply forgiving with our own strength and not with the power or strength of the Holy Spirit. Forgiveness must be done in the strength, power, and ability of God. God is the healer, not only of diseases, but also of our inner brokenness and wounds caused by the injustices of man.

If you are still struggling with bitterness or anger because of the things people have done to you, I strongly encourage you to turn your heart to the Word of God, for through His Word, God He is going to restore you once again. In Matthew 11:28, Jesus says, "Come to me, all who labor and are heavy laden, and I will give you rest" (ESV). When you surrender the heavy burden of your hurts, injustice, hatred, anger, bitterness, and unforgiveness to God, He cleanses your soul, mind, and body through His refreshing and renewing Spirit and gives you rest in His glorious presence. When you are overwhelmed by God's presence, there is no way you can remember or embrace your past pain because the new has come; you are a new creature who has been empowered to love as God loves, to forgive as God forgives, and to show mercy and grace to all humanity as He does. No, it is not easy to forgive and forget the injustices of man against us, but the love and power of God in us makes it possible.

Forgive—not with your emotions but with your heart and everything that is within you. Let no hurt rule over you, but rule over offense through the powerful weapon of forgiveness. We have all gone through trials, injustice, and offense, but thank God we are still here and still standing in His glorious presence because we live on the principles of God and not on our feelings or the traditions of man. In 2 Corinthians 4:8–11 Paul says this:

We are pressured in every way but not crushed; we are perplexed but not in despair; we are persecuted but not abandoned; we are struck down but not destroyed. We always carry the death of Jesus in our body, so that the life of Jesus may also be revealed in our body. For we who live are always given over to death because of Jesus, so that Jesus' life may also be revealed in our mortal flesh.

In His humanity Jesus was subject to offense, false accusations, trials, persecution, and even death, but all these did not crush Him down or destroy God's plan and purpose for His life. They did not put out the fire of God burning inside of Him. Jesus did not harbor bitterness toward those who persecuted Him, falsely accused Him, and insulted Him. Even from the cross, He said, "Father, forgive them, because they do not know what they are doing" (Luke 23:34). Has offense put out the fire of God in you? Or has opposition stopped you from pursuing God wholeheartedly? Has man's rejection taken you out of the presence of God or extinguished your zeal and passion for Jesus Christ? Come on! Rise up in the power of the living God who created you and called you to do His will, and put away every offense in your heart.

Effectual Forgiveness Is Heartfelt

Effectual forgiveness is powerful and genuine because it is heartfelt forgiveness, which is free of pretense or hypocrisy. Many times people will say they have forgiven such and such a person, and yet they continue to bring up the name of that person to others and talk about the person in a bad way. As long as you are bringing up past memories of what someone did to you or are inwardly disgusted when you see the person who offended you, know that you have not yet forgiven with your heart. You have not forgiven your offender until you can demonstrate a godly love toward that person and pray for him or her. Jesus said in Matthew 5:44, "But I tell you, love your enemies and pray for those who persecute you." The truth is you cannot pray for someone you have not first forgiven, and you cannot love someone you have not forgiven. Love demands forgiveness, and forgiveness calls for love.

Forgiving with one's emotions only is dangerous because it develops the culture of hypocrisy or falsehood in a person's life. The person ends up professing to have forgiven his or her offender while still being tormented by hatred or painful memories of the past. On several occasions Saul pretended to have "forgiven" David, and yet deep down in his heart he was plotting murder. It is very difficult to detect such falsehood because in most cases it is hidden behind a smile. The test of real forgiveness is found in the attitude or behavior a person has toward those he or she professes to have forgiven. And this test applies to us as much as it does to others.

If you have forgiven as you have been forgiven, you will be able to walk in love, to have patience with the person who offended you, and not feel envy when the Lord is blessing that person (1 Corinthians 13:4–8). You will not dishonor or demean the person in any way but will show kindness to him or her. Right now you might be whispering or silently saying to yourself, "My offender needs no forgiveness; he needs to pay for the wrongs done against me." Well, you are absolutely right! Every evil thing we have done and continue to do on a daily basis must be paid for—and that is a lot of wrongs to account for. Thank God for His Son, Jesus Christ, who paid for our sins and delivered us from its power and death. In the same manner, we who have experienced forgiveness for our many sins by God's grace and through the blood of Jesus Christ must extend grace to those who have wronged us and forgive their sins with no conditions attached.

Having and demonstrating a forgiving heart identifies us with the righteousness of God ("like Father, like son"). Unforgiveness is simply a display or manifestation of the spirit of self-righteousness—suggesting that *we* have never messed up—while forgiveness is an illustration of God's righteousness through us. Furthermore, forgiveness reveals one's depth of connection to God's own heart. Heartfelt forgiveness is what brings healing to a hurting soul and deliverance from the power of hatred and anger. If we can learn to forgive with our heart and not merely with our emotions, we will learn to love people as Christ loves them—unconditionally, without any strings attached. What makes Jesus' forgiveness so amazing is that He has forgiven *all* our sins from the depths of His heart, and the Bible says, "Therefore, if the Son sets you free, you really will be free" (John 8:36). Jesus doesn't remember your past mistakes, bring them up once in a while, or count them against you. When He declares freedom to you, you are free, and your past is totally wiped out. If Jesus Christ has forgiven you, don't burden yourself again through unforgiveness and become a slave of anger, bitterness, and hatred. You are a free person—free to love, free to forgive, and free to live life peacefully in the presence of God.

How Many Times Should We Forgive?

Now, you may be asking, "How many times should I forgive my spouse, my family, my friends, my brothers and sisters in the Lord, or even my enemy?" That is a very good question, and a very important one too. Thankfully, Jesus gave us the answer. Let us turn to Jesus' teaching on this subject in Matthew 18:21–35. Notice that Jesus' instruction came in response to a question Peter asked Jesus, a question to which Peter himself offered an answer: "Lord, how many times could my brother sin against me and I forgive him? As many as seven times?" (Matthew 18:21).

Peter's ideal of forgiving someone "seven times" wasn't all that bad compared to the three times that was popularly taught within Judaism.

Three times was considered sufficient to show a forgiving spirit; after that, there was no forgiveness for the offender. This teaching probably was drawn from scriptures like the following:

> *"God certainly does all these things two or three times to a man in order to turn him back from the Pit, so he may shine with the light of life."* (Job 33:29–30)
>
> *The* Lord *says: I will not relent from punishing Damascus for three crimes, even four, because they threshed Gilead with iron sledges.* (Amos 1:3)
>
> *The* Lord *says: I will not relent from punishing Israel for three crimes, even four, because they sell a righteous person for silver and a needy person for a pair of sandals.* (Amos 2:6)

Based on the teaching prevalent in his time, we can say Peter's ideal of forgiving an offender seven times was a much higher standard. To Jesus, however, even Peter's "generous" suggestion was not a kingdom ideal or a standard of how many times a kingdom person must forgive. Kingdom people live by kingdom principles and not by human traditions or worldly standards. Therefore, Jesus said to Peter, "I tell you, not as many as seven . . . but 70 times seven" (Matthew 18:22). He then went on to compare the kingdom of God to a king who wanted to settle accounts with his slaves (verses 23–35), which we discussed in the previous chapter.

Seventy Times Seven = Unlimited Forgiveness

Jesus was not talking about literally multiplying seventy by seven to reach the maximum limit on forgiving the offender. To take His words this way is to miss the kingdom principle Jesus was teaching. Jesus was teaching that in the kingdom of heaven, forgiveness is unlimited when true repentance is present. No one actually counts each time he or she is offended until "seventy times seven" is reached. That is insanity, and that is not what Jesus was teaching. The expression "seventy times seven" equals "unlimited forgiveness," because in the kingdom of God, forgiveness is endlessly available to anybody and everybody who repents and turns away from his or her wickedness. When we repent and ask for forgiveness from God, He forgives us, and He does not count our sins against us or keep a record of them. In the same way, we are to forgive other people without limits and without keeping a record of their sins against us. That is kingdom forgiveness and effectual forgiveness.

Similarly, Jesus said this in Luke 17:3–4:

"If your brother sins, rebuke him, and if he repents, forgive him. And if he sins against you seven times in a day, and comes back to you seven times, saying, 'I repent,' you must forgive him."

First, to rebuke in the above scripture doesn't mean we point out every sin we see; it simply means we bring sin to a person's attention with the purpose of restoring the person to God and to others. This must be done carefully, with a godly attitude and character, and in the spirit of humility and not in self-righteousness. When you are offended, don't be like the world and rush to tell everybody. Instead, go to the person and bring the wrong done to his or her attention so that any seeds of bitterness and anger can be uprooted. If the person is not approachable or does not want to talk about it, forgive on your part and let go of the offense so that you are not pulled into bitterness or unforgiveness. Above all, rebuke or correct a person in love and not in anger or to prove the person is wrong and you are right, which is the political attitude of the world. Kingdom people do things, not to prove they are right, but to bring honor and glory to the name of God and to repair any damage the enemy is trying to inflict upon God's people. Furthermore, your rebuke must always be tied to forgiveness; otherwise, it will never bring restoration to a sinning person or help your relationship.

Repentance and asking for forgiveness are extremely important because genuine repentance and forgiveness brings restoration. They mend any differences and bring people into fellowship with God or into a united fellowship with each other. It is unfortunate that some people today are teaching that we do not need repentance anymore. As a remnant of God who fear, honor, and respect God's holy name, we must not accept that kind of seduction and comfort by Satan. We are to repent if we realize we are living in sin so that we can maintain our fellowship and relationship with our holy, righteous, and living God. In the same way, if we realize we have sinned against anybody or each other, we must humble ourselves, repent, and ask for forgiveness so that we can walk and work in unity and peace together as one body of Christ.

Repentance Is Key to Effectual Forgiveness

Repentance, or turning from sin, is key to effectual forgiveness. Where there is true repentance, there is restoration, revival, and life. Never should we confuse God's ideal of making forgiveness available to us or to humanity while we were yet sinners with the ideal of our reaching out through faith and in repentance of our sins and accepting God's provision of forgiveness through Christ's death, accepting the Lord Jesus Christ as our King and Master and declaring Him to be Lord over our lives. When the Bible says, "While we were yet sinners, Christ died for us" (Romans 5:8), it simply means that through God's grace Christ paid the penalty for our sins. Our sins called for the death penalty, but Christ paid that sentence on our behalf, consequently delivering us from the power of sin and death. Today, forgiveness of sin is available to any willing soul ready to live in the presence of God. By making forgiveness of sin available to all humanity, God was demonstrating His love, grace, and mercy. Again, this does not mean all people of every nation are automatically saved from the power of sin and death. Each one of us needs salvation, and salvation comes by placing our faith in Christ; this in turn involves repentance, or leaving our worldly lifestyle, and embracing a new way of living as Christ lived.

Just prior to answering Peter's question and teaching about forgiving the offender without any limits, Jesus gave three steps to effectively dealing with a sinning brother. In Matthew 18:15–17 He said:

> *"[1] If your brother sins against you, go and rebuke him in private. If he listens to you, you have won your brother. [2] But if he won't listen, take one or two more with you, so that by the testimony of two*

or three witnesses every fact may be established. [3] If he pays no attention to them, tell the church. But if he doesn't pay attention even to the church, let him be like an unbeliever and a tax collector to you."

Nowhere in the Bible do we see Jesus teaching us to ignore, avoid, or forget offenses. Many of us are taught to ignore or forget them and move on. In reality, however, we do not forget and we do not move on because that pain or issue is stored in our hearts. In order for effectual forgiveness to take place, we cannot just ignore the problem or it will become the foundation of hatred and future problems. To clear away any offense or dispute or personal grievance, we first must go personally to the offending person and speak to him or her as Jesus said, rebuking the person in private (confidentially). If the offender does not listen and change his or her ways, we are to take one or two more witnesses and confront the person. Again, if there is no repentance, we are to tell the church, and if the offender does not listen even to the church, together we are to let that person be to us like an unbeliever.

People who refuse to repent, or change their evil ways, are not true believers, so you should let them be and move on. There are people who will respond by asking for forgiveness, and there are others who will never ask for forgiveness. Thus, if people ask for forgiveness, forgive them, and if they refuse to repent and ask for forgiveness, as a kingdom person, you are still to forgive them and move on. You will see your relationship and friendship restored with some people you forgive because they repent of their sins. And your relationship or friendship with others will not be restored, even though you forgive them, because they do not repent of their sins.

Repentance, which involves an acknowledgment of sin and a change of attitude, is crucial to the restoration of families, unity, and fellowship with one another. John the Baptizer preached, "Repent, because the kingdom of heaven has come near!" (Matthew 3:2). John's message focused on repentance, and Jesus emphasized the same thing from the outset of His ministry (Matthew 4:17). As people repent, they abandon their sinful lifestyles and thus allow God to exercise His kingdom rule and reign through them.

Repentance is not a weakness; it is an expression of humility before a holy God and before our fellow man. Where there is repentance, God withholds His judgment. A good example of how God withholds His judgment when people repent is found in God's dealings with the people of Nineveh. The Ninevites were very wicked people, and God was about to bring judgment upon them. Before doing so, however, He sent Jonah to preach against the city and warn them about the impending wrath of God. When Jonah finally preached against Nineveh and warned them about God's imminent punishment, the people repented. They believed in God and proclaimed a fast. They dressed in sackcloth, from the greatest of them to the least, as a sign of humility (Jonah 3:5). When God saw their repentant hearts and that they had turned away from their wickedness, He relented from sending disaster upon them.

We cannot emphasize enough the power of repentance. It causes God to withhold His judgment, and it brings us back on track with Him, both in fellowship and in relationship. Never be fooled into thinking you can go on living in sin without repentance and still maintain your fellowship with God or your position in the kingdom of God. There is no sin in God's kingdom. You must repent and change your ways. It is not a question of whether God loves you. He loves you unconditionally, but He doesn't love the sin that is in you. That sin will take you to hell if you do not repent.

Effectual forgiveness is a forgiveness that knows no limits or favoritism. It is a forgiveness that can be faithfully practiced only by kingdom-minded and kingdom-consumed people, people who are full of the Lord's love and full of the presence of God. Just as God's love knows no bounds, so the forgiveness that comes from that love is bigger than any offense or sin. Kingdom people operate in love, and their love for the lost and for each other always outmuscles offense. It was in this kind of forgiveness and love that Jesus and His most faithful followers operated. Their love for the lost and desire to reach them with the good news of the kingdom got them persecuted, beaten, and even killed, yet they did not hold a grudge against their persecutors but instead forgave them.

Is your love reserved only for people of a certain group or religion? Do you forgive people only when they make it up to you? That is a shallow level of forgiveness and not at the level of God's kingdom. God is calling on His people who have zeal and passion for His kingdom to love and forgive as He does. Now more than ever, true disciples of Jesus Christ must demonstrate their spiritual strength, maturity, and stability through the weapons of love, forgiveness, prayer, and praise and worship. If God lives in you and you truly love Him, prove it by your compassion for the lost and your love, not only for God almighty but also for His created people.

What the world needs today are passionate people of God who are filled with God's power, grace, and mercy and are sensitive to the Spirit of God. God wants to do something big in this world. The problem is that the people God wants to work in and through to accomplish His work are consumed with hatred, anger, bitterness, and the spirit of unforgiveness. We need reconciliation, humility, genuineness of faith, and love for God and for each other.

Jesus changed the world through unity with God the Father and the Holy Spirit and through the power of forgiveness. If we desire to change the world and are serious about it, the first step is forgiveness and reconciliation, which brings unity. When we have reconciled with each other and forgiven one another, we will accomplish much here on earth for the kingdom of God.

In our next and final chapter, we are going to look at the power of reconciliation created by a repentant heart and the cost of walking in unity. Walking in unity is, in fact, costly, but it makes a great impact.

Chapter 10

THE POWER OF RECONCILIATION

ONE OF THE GREATEST BENEFITS OF EFFECTUAL FORGIVENESS IS THAT IT PRODUCES the spirit of reconciliation; and where there is reconciliation, unity is birthed; and where there is unity, there is corporate anointing. Corporate anointing is one of the missing pieces of the puzzle in the body of Christ today. This is because it has been overshadowed by the spirit of unforgiveness we have been talking about. No doubt most of us desire to see the reviving fire of God invade the nations. We want to change the world, and we want to see God's kingdom and His will established here on earth through us. But what we must clearly understand, both individually and as the body of Christ, is that it is impossible for God to do what He desires to do in the nations with a divided community of believers.

With God working supernatural miracles through them, the early church did great damage to the kingdom of darkness. This was accomplished because they were united with God the Father, Jesus Christ, and the Holy Spirit, as well as with each other. There are things that God does powerfully through individuals, and there are even greater things He does through a united corporate body, the church. The ultimate goal of God for each individual is for that person to function within the support of a corporate body and become a catalyst, or spark, of "spiritual fire" to light up the entire body. Therefore, the individual needs the body, and likewise the body needs the individual to function to his or her full capacity in order to produce the desired results. The body, or church, then, is only as strong as the individuals who make up the body, but sadly, because of offense and indifference in the hearts of many individuals, the body is not functioning at its full potential or capacity.

In this generation, when evil and ungodliness seem to be increasing and influencing the actions of people all over the world, as believers in Christ we cannot afford to let unforgiveness or indifference stop us from establishing God's rule and reign in our communities. We need to be reconciled with the Godhead and with each other so that the Spirit of God can peacefully and powerfully work through us and break down the walls that prevent us from working together and igniting a fire of God in the world that can never be quenched.

Unity does not mean we totally agree with each other on every issue, but it does mean we totally agree with the Spirit of God and His Word and obediently do what He wants us to do; namely, bring lost souls into His kingdom and establish His peaceful reign. Unity is not looking alike, speaking alike, or dressing alike. Unity is an inner commitment to the culture of the kingdom of God and the Spirit of Jesus Christ. We are one because we all come from one spiritual Father—God the Father. We must stop looking at people's cultural backgrounds before we can love or accept them, but instead accept and love them because Christ has accepted them and we are one with them through His blood.

Unity calls for respect for a diversity of gifts and spiritual offices and for other people, regardless of their cultural background, nationality, or race. Furthermore, unity calls for honor, both for God and for each other. Honor and respect are key ingredients of unity, reconciliation, and peace. We cannot reconcile with others or work in unity with people or with God if we lack honor and respect for them. If we do not respect and honor God, we will not respect or honor kingdom things and other people. If we honor and respect God, we will also honor and respect other people and reconcile our differences with them because they are created in the image of God.

Reconciliation and unity are costly. They will cost us our self-importance, and they demand meekness, forgiveness, respect, and honor. But the benefits of unity and reconciliation are massive and sometimes unexplainable. After the people had marched around Jericho seven times, the walls of the city collapsed because the people were united both with each other and in their faith in the God of unity (Hebrews 11:30). Satan understands the shear gravity of unity, and this is why he tries by every possible means to divide God's people.

Throughout the Bible, God calls His people to live in unity with one another. The goal is that we all reach unity in the faith and in the knowledge of the Son of God and become mature, by the measure of the fullness of Christ (Ephesians 4:11–13). Unity is not an option but a command from God that we all must obey if we truly love God and desire to fulfill our heavenly callings. This is why the Bible puts such emphasis on unity (cf. 2 Chronicles 30:12; Psalm 133:1; John 17:22–23; Romans 12:4; 1 Corinthians 1:10; 12:12–13; Galatians 3:26–28; Ephesians 4:3; Colossians 3:13–15; 1 Peter 3:8).

Every one of us can admit it is not easy to work with others in unity, especially when we all come from different cultural backgrounds and have different mind-sets. Yet God calls us to walk and work together in unity—and this is possible. God is the Father of unity. The three persons of the Trinity—Father, Son, and Holy Spirit—work powerfully together in unity. And because we share in God's "DNA," we too can work powerfully as a united body without competition.

God's people work best in a united body. There is power in unity, but the question is this: How can we work together in unity? The answer is simple: By first getting rid of those things that stop us from working together in unity. Some of those things we have already looked at, such as unforgiveness, anger, bitterness, jealousy, and slander. But there is another powerful force that stops us from working in unity as the body of Christ, and it is a huge hindrance to reconciliation, peace, and stability. This force is a spirit of religious and political competitiveness . We need first to overcome this force in our lives and in our midst if we are to reconcile with each other and work powerfully as one united and anointed body of Christ.

Overcoming a Religiously and Politically Competitive Spirit

God has not called His people to compete with each other but rather to function in accordance with the grace, gifts, and abilities He has poured out upon each individual church. We are not anointed to outshine each other in gifts or callings but to work together in love and to rescue, mend, and bring healing to the lost. In most cases competition comes from the spirit of unforgiveness, offense, and jealousy. In God's eyes there are no gifts, talents, or callings that are unimportant. All gifts or ministries are important and crucial to the fulfillment of God's plans and purposes on the earth. We should never be angry when God uses other people differently than He uses us. Rather, we should embrace other gifts or ministries and support them through prayer and even financially so that they can fulfill their mandate. The first step or key to true reconciliation is putting away from our lives as individuals and as the body of Christ this competitive spirit that centers on religious and political concerns. We desperately need to overcome this evil force that has been taking over in churches if we are to walk in peace, unity, and the power of God. We cannot walk in unity unless we agree with each other and with what God wants to do through each one of us (Amos 3:3).

It is amazing that when a mosque or a Buddhist temple opens up in the neighborhood, no one in the Christian community seems to be bothered by it. However, when another church opens up or another gift or ministry emerges, it is showered with opposition and criticism from the Christian community. Why is this? It is because we have failed to understand God's culture of diversity and because of a competitive spirit that opposes everything God would like to do through each and every one He has called according to His grace. A competitive spirit within the church sees other churches and ministries as threats to its establishment and work. Even some of Jesus' disciples at one point had that kind of spirit, and Jesus had to correct them. Jesus had just finished correcting His disciples' thinking after they had been arguing about "who would be the greatest of them" (Luke 9:46–48). Then John suddenly brought up another issue: "Master, we saw someone casting out demons in Your name; and we tried to prevent him because he does not follow along with us" (verse 49 NASB). But Jesus responded to him and said, "Don't stop him . . . because whoever is not against you is for you" (verse 50).

A religiously and politically competitive spirit will try everything possible to stop others from doing the work of God because its desire is to be the only channel through which God reaches the world. Consequently, if God raises up other people or others rise up to do the work of God, those who possess such a competitive spirit will do everything possible to stop that work because they feel threatened. The disciples thought they were the only ones who were to cast out demons in the name of Jesus Christ. Any other people were not welcome. Jesus said no to that worldly mentality. He said, "Whoever is not against you is for you." To Jesus, the person who was casting out demons in His name was a disciple too, even though he wasn't officially following Jesus from town to town.

We don't have to agree on every issue in order to work together, and we don't have to come from the same congregation to work together. Those who are saved and born of the Spirit are not against us, as long as they are preaching true and sound doctrine in line with the gospel of the Lord Jesus Christ. They are not our enemies, and we should never be hostile toward them. Instead, we should support them in whatever way possible because they are doing what they are called to do according to the grace bestowed upon them by God. God has apportioned to each one of us a measure of grace, and we are to function in that grace if we are to be effective in what He has called us to do. Never should we compare our level of grace with that of others. We are to stay and operate within our gifts so that we can bring glory to God and avoid being consumed by the spirit of religious and political competitiveness that is prevalent in the world today.

A competitive spirit is very dangerous because ultimately it doesn't want to see the work of God advance or God's people blessed. In Genesis 26:12-22, we see this kind of spirit in operation. God blessed Isaac. Isaac was rich and kept getting richer until he was very wealthy, but the Philistines became envious (envy or jealousy is a sure sign of a competitive spirit), so they stopped up all the wells the servants of Isaac's father, Abraham, had dug by filling them with dirt. Then they ordered Isaac to leave, not because Isaac had done anything wrong, but simply because Isaac was "much too powerful" for them. Isaac, who was a man of peace and humility, left the place without fighting them and moved to a valley called Gerar and lived there. In Gerar, Isaac reopened the water wells that had been dug in the days of his father, Abraham, and that the Philistines had stopped up after Abraham died. But the herdsmen of Gerar quarreled with Isaac's herdsmen and said, "The water is ours!" Isaac named that place *Quarrel* because they quarreled with him.

Think about this for a moment: The wells were not in use before Isaac got there. In fact, Isaac's men had to dig them up again to reopen them. But a competitive and political spirit breeds jealousy and fights everything and anything. Isaac, again as a man of humility and peace, left with his men and dug another well. Unfortunately, again the herdsmen quarreled with him over that well too, so Isaac named it *Hostility*. Isaac again moved from there and dug another well. This time the quarrelsome and hostile people did not challenge him, and Isaac named it *Open Spaces* and said, "For now the Lord has made room for us, and we will be fruitful in the land" (Genesis 26:22).

How can we identify a religiously and politically competitive spirit? We recognize it by the fact that it is quarrelsome, hostile, boastful, and proud; it talks a lot but does little. And how can we identify a godly spirit? It is revealed through humility and patience. Isaac and Jesus were full of humility and patience. They could have fought back when they were attacked, but they did not because of their humility, patience, and desire for peace.

The account of Isaac presents a good example of what the competitive spirit looks like. Sadly, this spirit has found its way into the Christian world too through the spirit of jealousy and hatred. This spirit has destroyed many ministries and Christians and has hindered the progress of God's work in the nations. One of the challenges Jesus faced when He began His ministry, announcing the arrival of the kingdom of God and its influence, was a competitively minded people everywhere He went. They opposed Him, quarreled with Him, and were extremely hostile toward Him and His ministry because they felt threatened. They feared the collapse of their religious system and traditions. For this reason they successfully called for His crucifixion. Just like the Philistines, who asked Isaac to leave because they considered him too powerful, the religious leaders of Jesus' day had Jesus crucified because they considered Him a threat to the religious establishment and their position, authority, and status in the community.

A competitive spirit centered on political and religious concerns is quarrelsome and hostile to the things of God and to the people of God. Just as Jesus and Isaac responded to this spirit in humility by moving from one place to another when they were opposed, we are to respond in a similar manner. Humility is not a weakness. It is the character of the peaceful and a trait of the godly. As He gave them a charge to go and preach the good news of the kingdom, Jesus taught His disciples, "If anyone will not welcome you or listen to your words, shake the dust off your feet when you leave that house or town" (Matthew 10:14). The disciples were not to fight or shove the gospel down the throats of the people or fight to be in a particular house or town. The world is too big for that. There are numerous people all over who are thirsty for the refreshing and renewing word of God.

Why did Jesus tell His disciples to shake the dust off their feet if a city or home did not welcome them? Well, pious Jews of Jesus' day often shook the dust from their feet to show their separation from Gentile practices; so if the disciples shook the dust of a Jewish town from their feet, it would show their separation from Jews who rejected their Messiah. This gesture was not done in bitterness or anger but to show the people they were making a tragic mistake in choosing to reject the gospel of truth; it essentially marked them as pagans.

When you are rejected or opposed, you don't have to be resentful, bitter, or angry about it. Move on to another place as the Holy Spirit gives you guidance, and the Lord will provide you with "open spaces." Then you shall say, as Isaac said, "For now the Lord has made room for us, and we will be fruitful in the land" (Genesis 26:22). When you have this kind of attitude and character, you will not do things to please man or to be seen by man or to compete with anybody. You will walk in peace and humility. And where there is humility, there is forgiveness and reconciliation.

The greatest obstacle to the work of God today is a politically and religiously competitive spirit. This spirit manufactures division, individualism, self-centeredness, and insecurity. It also causes many people to be self-focused and concerned and consumed with their outward religious appearance rather than their spiritual function and impact. God does not measure our ministry success by our outward performance or display but by the impact and transformation He is able to effect through us upon a community or upon a person's life. God has not given out His anointing to us so that we can put on a show of faith and become well known. We are not in "show business"; we are in the business of winning souls by utilizing all the powerful weapons and gifts God has provided to us through different individuals and churches. If God's people could fully grasp this truth and run with it, the kingdom of darkness would have no power or influence upon our communities, and the church would be a place of God's fire.

Whenever you feel like competing with another person or you feel envy when God is using other people or ministries in a mighty way, stop and say to yourself, "I am called to something different than they are. They are not a threat to me. We are all connected to the kingdom of God, so I will support what they are doing."

Never speak ill of other ministries or churches in your community or compare your local assembly to another assembly, because these things are not important. We are not in competition with one another but are one in our Messiah. Let others play their roles in the kingdom of God, and play yours with all your strength, ability, and passion. Be the best at what you do, not because you want to compete with others, but because you want to release the power of God in your circles of influence with everything within you. And finally, don't feel intimidated by the skills, talents, or gifts of others. Instead, complement them, and others will complement yours. When you do this, it is easy to reconcile with others because you are not in competition with them but in oneness with them. Let the rains of God's spirit of reconciliation pour over you and help you to effectively overcome and overpower the evil force of a competitive spirit that binds people from walking in peace, reconciliation, and forgiveness.

Reconciliation Is Costly

Talk is cheap; action is extremely expensive. We can read, talk, and preach about reconciliation, but if we take no action, we will never be reconciled to others or walk in peace. Politicians and churches talk and preach about reconciliation in the nations or in the community, but they seldom take a step forward to effect it. Why is this? It is because reconciliation is costly. It costs a person his or her self-importance and pride because in order to be reconciled to another, one has to humble or lower oneself, and very few are willing to do that. It is the same with forgiveness. One has to give up his or her position or feelings in order to forgive another person. In other words, one has to humble oneself and forgive, regardless of the damage done by the offender. In addition, reconciliation is expensive because it means setting aside personal demands to be heard or to do things a certain way. To understand how costly reconciliation of a broken friendship or relationship is, let us again turn to Matthew 5:23–24.

> *"If you are offering your gift on the altar, and there you remember that your brother has something against you, leave your gift there in front of the altar. First go and be reconciled with your brother, and then come and offer your gift."*

Jesus was instructing His disciples to seek reconciliation, even if it meant one must stop in the middle of offering a sacrifice at the temple and leave the sacrifice at the altar. If someone remembered that his brother had a grievance against him or that he had suffered an offense at the hands of his brother, he was to go to that person and seek reconciliation before offering his sacrifice. In reality, this could require a lengthy trip from the Jerusalem temple to reconcile with his brother before returning to complete his sacrifice at the altar. Yet he had to pay that price because he could not afford to offer something to God and not have it accepted by God.

How many times have we offered or presented our sacrifice of praise, worship, prayer, or money to God when we were full of resentment, bitterness, or anger and knew fully well we had a grievance in our heart that needed to be settled? This is why we give to God but do not see the return or fruits of our giving. We give for the sake of giving and without a reverential fear of God; thus, we are not offering Him a sacrifice that is pure and unblemished. There is a cost to reconciliation. We must be willing to go the extra mile and surrender our self-importance by humbling ourselves and asking for forgiveness, even if we did not purposely or knowingly offend the other person, so that we can uproot from our heart all the seeds of hurt, offense, hatred, bitterness, and anger and walk in peace with both God and man. Too many relationships, including marriages, are totally destroyed because the parties involved are unwilling to humble themselves and forgive or ask for forgiveness. Yet with humility we can restore our relationship with others and walk in the power of God.

No, not all relationships can be restored, but on our part and as believers in Christ we must make every effort to settle disputes with others (Luke 12:58) and to walk in peace with all humanity (Matthew 5:9) so that we can demonstrate to the world we are indeed true sons and daughters of God. We are to be tenderhearted, gentle, and kind and not harsh or unpleasant because we are God's people and thus His light and salt to this world. We must not wait on the other person to ask for forgiveness or seek restoration of our relationship or friendship; we should make the first move and be a peacemaker. Let us owe nothing to anyone, except to love them (Romans 13:8); let us show them the graciousness of God through our lives. With the power of reconciliation, we can advance the kingdom of God and see God work miracles in our midst like never before. Indeed, the secret of walking in the power and presence of God lies in walking in the spirit of forgiveness and unity.

Walking and Living in Peace Depends on Us

Walking and living in peace with other members of the body depends on us. We have the power to choose peace or strife through our actions and attitudes. Romans 12:18 says, "If it is possible, as far as it depends on you, live at peace with everyone" (NIV). We cannot control the attitudes or actions of others, but surely we can let God control ours. Just because someone treats us badly or does not respect us does not mean we should do the same to them, and just because someone has offended us does not mean we should offend them too. We must choose to be people with a different spirit, and when we do, God will use us mightily. It is time for us to let go of every offense and resentment in our heart and forgive so that we do not let anger discourage us from loving people or illustrating the heart of God to those who oppose or persecute us. God is raising up a new generation of men and women who have the spirit of Jesus Christ, Abraham, Isaac, and many more powerful characters of the Bible. He is raising up a people full of love, peace, and humility, a people with a passion and zeal for what God is passionate about—lost souls.

Conclusion

FORGIVENESS IS A POWERFUL WEAPON, BUT IT HAS BEEN UNDERUTILIZED, PERHAPS BECAUSE many perceive it to be an expression of weakness or a useless exercise. Yet God used the weapon of forgiveness in the victorious redemption of humanity from the kingdom of darkness. And if you would like to have back what the enemy has stolen from you, or you would like to mend everything the enemy has broken in your life, then you too need to use the spiritual weapon of forgiveness. Through Jesus Christ, God used the weapon of forgiveness to redeem a people Satan had stolen away. Scripture tells us that when Yohannan (John), also called John the Baptist, saw Jesus Christ, all he could say was, "Here is the Lamb of God, who takes away the sin of the world! This is the One I told you about: 'After me comes a man who has surpassed me, because He existed before me'" (John 1:29–30). Jesus was equipped to win back lost souls, not with swords or shields, but with the weapon of forgiveness. He was sent by God to pardon the sins of the people and loose them from the bondage, or chains, of its power. He did not enter into a boxing match or physical confrontation with Satan. All He did was forgive and heal the brokenhearted.

Micah 7:18–19 records these great words about God:

Who is a God like you, pardoning iniquity and passing over transgression for the remnant of his inheritance? He does not retain his anger forever, because he delights in steadfast love. He will again

> *have compassion on us; he will tread our iniquities underfoot. You will cast all our sins into the depths of the sea.* (ESV)

God's weapon against Satan is forgiveness, and the Bible clearly proves this fact. There is no one under the sun or in the heavens who is so willing or able to forgive or show mercy like our God. We do not forgive like God because we have not yet sufficiently developed the culture of God's nature in us and fully appreciated His forgiveness of our sins or known the effectiveness of the weapon of forgiveness in the spiritual realm.

God's weapon of forgiveness is free and available to all, but there are conditions to fully walk in it. One condition is our willingness to receive forgiveness freely from Him. Another condition required to receive God's forgiveness is repentance, which involves confession and turning away from wickedness. God requires humans to turn from their sinful ways and turn to Him as a sign of humility and acceptance of His forgiveness. Isaiah 55:7 says, "Let the wicked forsake his way, and the unrighteous man his thoughts; let him return to the Lord, that he may have compassion on him, and to our God, for he will abundantly pardon" (ESV). And 1 John 1:9 also states, "If we confess our sins, he is faithful and just to forgive us our sins and to cleanse us from all unrighteousness" (ESV). God is more than ready to offer forgiveness to a repentant sinner. God's forgiveness is limitless and His love is unconditional, but people must repent of their sins to receive total restoration. Ephesians 1:7–8 shows us that forgiveness of sin is secured by undeserved, unmerited grace through the purchase price of Jesus' physical death: "In him we have redemption through his blood, the forgiveness of our trespasses, according to the riches of his grace" (ESV). Colossians 1:14 says the same thing. So why is repentance so important, both in the restoration of our relationship with God and in restoration of relationships with one another? It is because repentance dismantles the walls that prevent us from living in fellowship with God and man.

Confession and repentance of sin in relation to both God and each other is important to the effectiveness of the weapon of forgiveness in our lives. Throughout the Bible we see that when people confessed their sins and repented, God forgave them and restored His presence upon them. Here are a few scriptures that show us that:

- "'In accordance with your great love, forgive the sin of these people, just as you have pardoned them from the time they left Egypt until now.' The LORD replied, 'I have forgiven them, as you asked'" (Numbers 14:19–20 NIV).
- "Then David said to Nathan, 'I have sinned against the LORD.' Nathan replied, 'The LORD has taken away your sin. You are not going to die'" (2 Samuel 12:13 NIV).
- "If my people, who are called by my name, will humble themselves and pray and seek my face and turn from their wicked ways, then I will hear from heaven, and I will forgive their sin and will heal their land" (2 Chronicles 7:14 NIV).

As we study the forgiving heart of God, we see God's power on display. Through the offense of sin committed by Adam and Eve, humanity was spiritually dead, under God's wrath, enslaved to the Devil, and following their own evil thoughts. Human beings had become God's enemies. Satan thought he had won the battle by turning people against God through the power of sin, but through the mighty weapon of forgiveness, God provided the way for them to be alive with Christ, to be raised up with Christ to glory, and to become free in Christ and have a seat in His presence. Thus, Satan lost the battle. He was overpowered through the blood of Jesus Christ that was shed on the cross because of the forgiving heart and grace of God. Forgiveness is still a force and a weapon Satan cannot withstand or conquer. Once a person forgives, Satan loses his grip on people, on marriages, and on the body of Christ.

Never allow fear, shame, or pride to stop you from seeking forgiveness for any wrongs you have committed, and never withhold forgiveness from others, whether they ask for it or not. Forgive, and as you forgive, the windows of heaven will be opened to pour out God's blessings over your life. Stand ready to use your weapon of forgiveness and recover everything the enemy has stolen from you.

There is no any other weapon that can release people from the chains of Satan as forgiveness does. Why? If you have forgiven your enemies, you will have the power to pray for them, love them, and help them. And if there is no hatred, bitterness, anger, resentment, or unforgiveness in you, the power and anointing of God will move in you and cause you to do greater works for God. Many people do not see the Holy Spirit use them or move through them because the spirit of unforgiveness has poisoned them. It is time for a spiritual detox. Release all the poison of unforgiveness, and the anointing of God will flow from you like a spring of pure and living water.

It is very important to understand that in life you will go through various challenges: trials, tribulations, persecution, and opposition. Knowing how to respond to these challenges will save your life, help you maintain your kingdom authority, and keep you from falling into the enemy's trap. Never respond to offense by taking it too personally. Instead, respond in humility and through the power of forgiveness. The kingdom of darkness has unleashed the power of offense upon the earth today. Everywhere you look, you will see offended and resentful people. God wants to unleash the weapon of forgiveness in His power so that the plans of Satan can be defeated. Satan wants to offend you so that he can entrap you and take you away from the presence of God. So guard your heart, and leave no room there for unforgiveness or anger to grow.

Furthermore, do not allow yourself to be one through whom offense comes but let your attitude, actions, and words be influenced by the Spirit of God. As an ambassador of Christ, never let the Devil use you to bring offense to others through gossip, criticism, or slander because these are stumbling blocks the Devil uses to discourage people from coming to Christ or living for Him. Romans 14:13, says, "Therefore, let us no longer criticize one another. Instead decide never to put a stumbling block or pitfall in your brother's way." Anyone who claims to be a man or woman of God and yet scatters and harms God's people is not a true servant of God or disciple of Jesus Christ. True servants of God and disciples of Jesus Christ do not cause others to fall and do not scatter God's people; rather they win people to God and help them grow to spiritual maturity.

As you forgive those who have offended you, God will forgive your sins and give you a breakthrough in life. When I personally discovered the power of forgiveness, I discovered what God wanted to do through me—to use me as a pure vessel, free from the toxin of bitterness and anger. I recovered my anointing. Satan tried to get me off track in my early years as a minister through offense, opposition, and rejection, but God spoke to me clearly and said, "Get rid of all your hurts, bitterness, and anger because you have been rejected so that I can accept you. You have been offended so that I can offer you a new life and spirit in My kingdom, a life of setting people free from the influence of Satan through unforgiveness." Today I minister with kingdom love, mercy, passion, and compassion for the hurting. No offense, no persecution, no injustice, no defamation, and no opposition can or will stop me from living for God and doing His work. I have forgiven all my offenders, and I will continue to forgive those who may offend me in the future, so that I can maintain my focus on God and not on the worldly things of this present life.

In conclusion, beware of the weapons Satan uses constantly to make people stumble in their faith and work for God and ministry to others: sin, pride, anger, unbelief, offense, and unforgiveness. Avoid these at all costs. Never allow Satan to bully you into sin because of offense, unforgiveness, or hurt. Allow the Holy Spirit of God to cleanse you of all hatred, anger, and bitterness in your heart so that you can serve God without any restrictions or limitations. You are called to excel in your service for God and to thrive in His glorious power. Forgive today, and your blessings and breakthrough will be unveiled. This is your time to shine with the presence of God. Let nothing stand in your way or stop you from doing exactly that.

About the Author

EVANGELIST REV. DR. KAZUMBA CHARLES WAS BORN IN CHINGOLA, THE BIBLE-BELT PROVINCE of Zambia. This former soccer player grew up as a troublesome young man who had no hope of living a hopeful and Spirit-filled life, but that changed dramatically in 1999. After being inspired and influenced to serve the Lord by his mother, a powerful intercessor, Kazumba encountered the power and presence of the living God that radically changed his life. He immediately began passionately pursuing the kingdom of God.

Dr. Kazumba is happily married to Glory, a beautiful and powerful woman of God. The Lord has blessed them with three wonderful, God-loving kids. Evangelist Kazumba and his wife, Glory, are a powerful team who have dedicated their lives to sharing the good news of the kingdom, winning souls for the kingdom of God, and bringing reformation and revival around the world. The Kazumbas are loving, caring, humble servants of God who are passionate about expressing the compassion of Jesus Christ for the lost, the broken, the sick, and those in captivity.

Evangelist Dr. Kazumba is an ordained and licensed minister in Canada. He is a dynamic preacher of the Word of God who travels around the globe to preach the gospel of Jesus Christ at crusades, seminars, and conferences. Dr. Kazumba has authored two other powerful and life-changing books, *Revisiting the Foundations* and *The Parables of the Kingdom*. He is the founder of an international evangelistic ministry called Christ Passion Evangelistic Network.

To learn more about Evangelist Dr. Kazumba, please visit www.kazumbacharles.com.

Printed in the USA
CPSIA information can be obtained
at www.ICGtesting.com
CBHW031119231023
1466CB00004B/119